Backcountry Fishing A GUIDE FOR
Hikers, Paddlers, and Backpackers

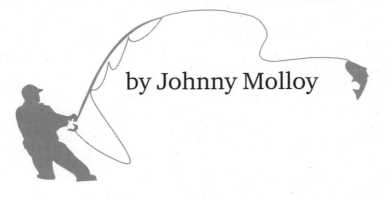

by Johnny Molloy

MENASHA RIDGE PRESS   Birmingham, Alabama

Published by Menasha Ridge Press
Printed in the United States of America
Distributed by Publishers Group West
First edition, first printing
Cover design by Travis Bryant
Text design by Barbara Williams
Cover photographs © Emilio Ereza/Alamy (top),
  © Alaska Stock, LLC/Alamy (bottom)
Interior photographs by Johnny Molloy except as follows:
  Mark Carroll, pages 25, 50, 154; John Cox, pages 18, 146; Scott Davis, page 1;
  Tina Dean, page 126; Kent Roller, page 43
Author photograph by Lynette Barker
Illustrations by Scott McGrew (pages 20–21 by Aaron Marable)
Indexing by Sylvia Coates

 Printed on recycled paper

Library of Congress Cataloging-in-Publication Data

Molloy, Johnny, 1961–
Backcountry fishing: a guide for hikers, paddlers,
  and backpackers/by Johnny Molloy. —1st ed.
    p. cm.
ISBN-13: 978-0-89732-650-6
ISBN-10: 0-89732-650-4
1. Fishing. 2. Outdoor recreation. I. Title.
SH441.M557 2008
799.1'1—dc22
                        2007042208

Menasha Ridge Press
P.O. Box 43673
Birmingham, Alabama 35243
www.menasharidge.com

Backcountry Fishing

Other books by Johnny Molloy

A Canoeing and Kayaking Guide to Kentucky (with Bob Sehlinger)
A Falcon Guide to Mammoth Cave National Park
A Paddler's Guide to Everglades National Park
Adventures on the Florida Trail
Beach and Coastal Camping in Florida
Beach and Coastal Camping in the Southeast
The Best in Tent Camping: The Carolinas
The Best in Tent Camping: Colorado (with Kim Lipker)
The Best in Tent Camping: Florida
The Best in Tent Camping: Georgia
The Best in Tent Camping: Kentucky
The Best in Tent Camping: Southern Appalachian and Smoky Mountains
The Best in Tent Camping: Tennessee
The Best in Tent Camping: West Virginia
The Best in Tent Camping: Wisconsin (with Kevin Revolinski)
Canoeing and Kayaking Florida (with Elizabeth F. Carter, Lou Glaros,
     John Pearce, and Doug Sphar)
Day and Overnight Hikes: Great Smoky Mountains National Park
Day and Overnight Hikes: Kentucky's Sheltowee Trace
Day and Overnight Hikes: Shenandoah National Park
Day and Overnight Hikes: West Virginia's Monongahela National Forest
50 Hikes in the North Georgia Mountains
50 Hikes in the Ozarks
50 Hikes in South Carolina
Fishing Tennessee
From the Swamp to the Keys: A Paddle through Florida History
Hiking Mississippi
Hiking the Florida Trail: 1,100 Miles, 78 Days, and Two Pairs of Boots
The Hiking Trails of Florida's National Forests, Parks, and Preserves
     (with Sandra Friend)
Land between the Lakes Outdoor Recreation Handbook
Long Trails of the Southeast
Paddling Georgia
Paddling Tennessee
60 Hikes within 60 Miles: San Antonio and Austin (with Tom Taylor)
60 Hikes within 60 Miles: Nashville
Trial by Trail: Backpacking in the Smoky Mountains

Visit the author's Web site: **www.johnnymolloy.com**

Table of Contents

Why Do It?

The morning had turned into afternoon and a thunderstorm drenched us. We were fishing for pike and bass on the shoreline of Basswood Lake in Minnesota, which forms the boundary with Canada. Earlier in the day a pike had broken my rod with a vicious strike, but now we were paddling toward our next campsite. The sun split the clouds, and filtering beams reflected off the water. Ahead we saw a dark speck. Paddling closer, the speck moved. I got out my binoculars—a bear was swimming across the lake! Slowly but surely the beast bruin-paddled from the Canadian side of the lake to the American side, right before our eyes. That night we sat before the flames, reliving our wildlife sighting, barely mentioning the broken pole. That is the backcountry fishing experience.

Fishing can be easy, if you want it to be—just drive to the local body of water, hop out of the vehicle, and start casting. Or launch a boat and motor, then zoom to the local honey hole. So why would anyone want to walk a trail to fish, or paddle a canoe or kayak to throw in a line, or carry a loaded backpack with them, often leaving for days at a time, fishing in a primitive setting? The answer lies in the overall experience, of which fishing is the central activity. This desire to match a scenic setting while matching wits with our finned friends is what separates the backcountry angler from the ordinary fisher.

Matching a scenic setting while matching wits with fish is the essence of backcountry fishing.

Introduction

Backcountry fishing separates you from the crowds, from those anglers literally unwilling to take the extra step, to leave the pavement or the powerboat to go head-to-head with swimming creatures lurking under the fluid waters that reflect the lands around them. And when fishing fever strikes, there is only one cure. If you are in such a state, why not go in a superlative setting? Why not go backcountry fishing?

For many of us, the lure of fishing is not always the fish, but the places where the fish are. Tossing a rod is just the excuse to get past the parking lot to enter the backcountry; to follow a foot trail tracing an Appalachian trout stream beneath a shady forest canopy, or cast for bass along a sun-splashed Ozark river, where inviting gravel bars offer campsites below magnificent bluffs; to trace a Rocky Mountain watercourse as it winds through a meadow flanked by majestic snowcapped peaks; to see what lies under the froth of a Sierra tributary flowing along granite banks; to paddle through a winding mangrove maze in the Everglades, casting for salty species inhabiting that unique slice of America.

This guide covers backcountry fishing, whether day-tripping in a canoe, day-hiking along a remote river, going for a multiday excursion in Quetico Provincial Park of Ontario or a weeklong backpack-fish fest in the Gila Wilderness of New Mexico. Whether you fly-fish, spin-fish, or saltwater-fish, with this book in hand you will be prepared not only for how to catch fish in the outback but how to be best prepared for backcountry fishing excursions.

Getting in the Backcountry

Whether you go by foot or by self-propelled craft, such as a canoe or kayak, backcountry travel leads anglers from an auto-accessible trailhead or put-in to a fishing destination they must reach on their own, without a car or motorboat. The simplest way to get there is by foot. Walking or hiking to the destination requires merely a trail and a body of water, whether it be a lake or stream. You may choose to go on a day trip or backpack for several days. Outback travel by boat is a little more complicated. A canoe or kayak is needed. In this situation, backcountry anglers start at a put-in and if by river, travel downstream, maybe camping, maybe not, and finish at a takeout. Other times, anglers will start and end in the same place, especially when traveling lakes, or a series of lakes connected by portages. Many kayaking destinations will be in salt water.

Backcountry anglers can explore such scenic destinations as Alaska's Chugach National Forest.

Weight and Space

Weight and space separate backcountry fishing from the ordinary fishing excursion. If taking a bass boat on the local reservoir for the day, you will likely take the kitchen sink along. Or if bait-fishing from a river bank accessible by car, you can take whatever you want, including a jar of pickled pig's feet to dine on. However, if backcountry bass-fishing Virginia's New River, you can bring only what'll fit in a canoe, or if back-pack fly-fishing Wyoming's Bridger-Teton Wilderness, you want to use weight and space efficiently.

Backcountry Decision-making

The first determination is which kind of fish I want to catch. This will determine the equipment to use. Say I'm going for cutthroat trout on Slough Creek in Yellowstone National Park. I'll be hiking a mostly open path to reach a stream that meanders through open meadows. This tells me I can use a longer rod and won't have to worry as much about storing and transporting it before reaching the creek. Once on the creek, I'll be able to walk along the meadows and fish from gravel bars that lie on the inside of the stream bends. It's summer, so I'll wear hiking shoes that can double as fishing shoes and bring a light jacket in case of a thunderstorm. In my day pack I'll carry a lunch and my camera for the many scenic shots available.

I'm going to catch and release fish, so I won't be carrying a creel or other means of keeping fish. Slough Creek has many pools and slack areas between faster sections. It is primarily populated with cutthroat trout, which are a lesser fighting cold-water fish. This is a good fly-fishing venue. It has a good insect population, and I will use a dry fly with a grasshopper pattern to watch the spectacle of a cutthroat rising to strike. I'll have plenty of casting room, with no overhead obstructions, and will be able to run the fly for relatively long distances down the stream.

Now, say I'm going trout-fishing on a small and overgrown stream of the Cohutta Wilderness in the North Georgia Mountains. I will be hiking a less maintained, thickly vegetated trail to access the stream. This tells me to use a shorter, two-piece rod (under five feet) and to carry it in my hand while walking or keep it well stowed while trekking between the trailhead and the stream access. It's spring, and the weather is variable, so I'll keep a fleece jacket and a rain jacket in my day pack. Because the stream is overgrown, I will likely have to wade nearly the whole time. So I'll bring lightweight felt-soled fishing shoes for in the water and wear some sturdy hiking boots with ankle support to reach the stream access. I'll cast ultra-light ¼- to ⅛-ounce spinners. Because the keepers of legal size on this tiny stream are rare I will not carry any fish-holding gear.

Such are the types of decisions to make while backcountry fishing, to which you will find answers in this book. We will go through the whats (what rod, what tackle, what lures, what techniques), the hows (proven techniques for locating and catching fish in the outback), and the wheres (a list of suggested destinations begins on page 141).

What Is Backcountry Fishing?

~ It's acrobatically stepping up a rocky stream under dark green tunnels with shafts of sunlight illuminating trout pools.

> ~ It's throwing your lure from the beach and watching a snook hit it with a vengeance and then burst upward toward the sky, landing on its side with the crash.

> ~ *It's having your line snap at precisely the wrong moment on Maine's Allagash River.*

~ It's dropping a Floating Rapala over a spawning bed and watching two smallmouth bass get hooked at once.

> ~ It's walking up the canyons of the Middle Fork Gila River with stone spires rising on their edges as you fish translucent waters for Gila trout and smallmouth bass.

> ~ It's reaching the gravel bar campsite with bragging rights for the biggest fish of the day.

~ It's quickly reeling in your fish as the boat turns sideways before hitting a partially submerged tree.

> ~ *It's drifting a fly down Panther Creek in June and catching a fish in front of the other anglers who have been shut out.*

~ It's planning on eating fish that night and returning to camp empty-handed only to find everyone else got shut out, too.

> ~ It's floating down the Namekogan River and catching smallmouth bass with a Red Mepps spinner while remarking on the North Woods scenery.

> ~ It's coming back to camp with stream-numbed feet and a rain-soaked upper half and getting straight into your sleeping bag to warm up.

~ It's standing on a granite point while watching the sunset and remarking on all the northern pike you caught from the lake below.

 ~ It's going above your knees in muck while carrying a canoe over your head on a mosquito-laden portage.

 ~ *It's catching your first fish on your first cast in an unfished high country lake.*

~ It's standing on a gravel bar with miles of meadow stretching before you while landing a trout against a backdrop of snowcapped mountains.

 ~ It's standing in crystal-clear water and finding a pair of hemostats glittering at your feet.

 ~ It's returning to camp to find your friend already has a fire going and is boiling water for coffee.

~ *It's casting spinners into a small coastal stream flowing off golden hills into the Pacific Ocean and catching rainbow trout.*

 ~ It's getting away from the noise, concrete, and cell phones while enjoying the serenity of nature.

 ~ It's feasting on fresh bass fillets while you sit in your camp chair as the last bit of daylight reflects off the water.

~ It's having a moose trot directly through your campsite on Wyoming's Salt River.

 ~ It's walking back to camp on a day as dark as night while thunder rolls overhead and it rains so hard you can't get any wetter.

 ~ It's searching for a good campsite after floating and fishing during a long, hot day and not finding one until nearly dark.

~ It's pulling plate-sized panfish from a Southern blackwater river and reeling them in from your kayak.

~ It's heaving your line as far out as you can and watching the lure get hit by trout swimming the clear waters of an alpine lake.

~ *It's preparing the coals just right to cook your fresh trout.*

~ It's wrapping your line around a tree and having your fly overhang a likely deep hole.

~ It's fishing a stream in Arizona that you can straddle and still pull out fish.

~ It's standing there with your buddy on a snow-fed lake and each catching a fish cast after cast after cast.

~ It's staying an extra day at the same campsite because the fishing is so good.

~ It's running out of lures toward the end of the trip while your friend is still slaying them with his last lure of that type.

~ *It's reeling in brook trout while framed in fall's kaleidoscope of colors.*

~ It's discovering a new lure that works.

~ It's desperately trying a new lure that doesn't work while in the midst of a shutout.

~ It's coming up an inch too short for the keeper limit.

~ It's floating down a beautiful river and wondering why you can't do this all the time.

~ It's floating down the river and doing it as much as you can.

~ It's backcountry fishing.

Backcountry Fishing Tackle

Getting a good-quality rod and reel is important. The backcountry is no place for cheap tackle. On the other hand, backcountry fishing is hard on gear, so don't buy something so expensive that you have to baby it, or worse yet, leave it at home.

The Rod

Selecting a rod, especially fly-fishing rods, can be overwhelming. Backcountry anglers will generally be searching out lightweight, sensitive, yet fairly tough rods. Consider action, responsiveness, and power. Action is the flexibility of the rod. The faster the action, the more sensitive the rod is, and the closer to the tip the rod bends. Responsiveness is how the rod releases energy stored in the cast and how fast the rod responds under the weight of a fish. The lighter the rod the more responsive it is. Power is the ability to lift the fish from the water. The heavier the rod, the more power it has. So when choosing a rod, think of the type of fish you're after. Say I'm going for sea trout in the Mississippi Gulf Islands, using plugs with multiple treble hooks. A medium weight, medium action six-foot rod will work here. It will have enough action to set the hook, enough responsiveness for long casts and handling runs, and finally, enough power to bring the fish home. When in doubt, always go with lighter rods for maximum sporting adventure.

Rod Material

Graphite is easily the most popular rod material these days. Graphite rods are not 100 percent graphite, but a composite of graphite and other materials, namely fiberglass. Making these graphite rods is complicated and involves a lot of heat, but suffice it to say there are ways to make a cheap graphite rod and an expensive one. It's a matter of getting what you pay for. A cheap rod is going to perform cheaply, and possibly break, whereas a well-made rod will serve well for years and perhaps save you

Consider action, responsiveness, and power when you choose a fishing rod.

from buying several cheap rods during the same time period. Some fly rods are still made of natural materials, such as bamboo. However, continually improving technology is leading to more composite rods. But being on the front end of new technology has a cost. The newest rods are quite expensive.

When choosing a fly rod consider its flex action. A tip-flex rod is stiffer, bending only one third of the way down the rod. It is less forgiving but allows farther casts. A midflex rod bends farther into the rod and is a better choice for beginning fly-fishers. A full-flex rod does as its name implies, bending the entire length of the rod. These are used when casting accuracy is more important than casting distance. Damping is the term used to describe how quickly a fly rod's tip stops vibrating after it is cast: the more vibration, the less accurate the rod is while casting.

Size of Rod

Rod size depends on the water you plan to fish and what kind of fish you seek. I almost always use a two-piece rod for packability. And packability starts when I leave the house and load the car. Virtually all backcountry fishing begins with a trip in the car. Be careful when loading your rod. I admit to using one-piece rods while on day-float trips near home. A two-piece rod will stow on a backpack much better and safer than a one piece. A one-piece rod tied onto a backpack will find every limb between the trailhead and the campsite. First, I keep my two-piece rods bound together with light cord or metal twist ties, covering the end tippet with a bandanna, which prevents it from getting broken off or bent to the point of breaking if it catches an errant limb. Other people stow the lower end of the two-piece rod in the pack, with the top sticking out of the pack. Still others store them in rod cases attached to the pack. In any case, it's important to keep the tip of the rod covered.

While paddling, a two-piece is not so critical, though a one-piece rod still has to survive the car trip. I have seen rods broken between the house and the water—the look on my friend John Cox's face is forever imprinted after he loaded a brand-new rod in the back of my Jeep, then flipped the passenger seat back and immediately broke the new rod; also the anger of my dad when I rolled up the window on a couple of rods sticking out, cracking them enough to make them unusable. Two-piece rods can be handy on portages, or if you want to store an extra one not being used while paddling. A two-piece rod will stow away much better in a kayak than a one piece.

Still others prefer multipiece cased rods. These certainly make sense as far as portability. However, the more pieces there are the more pieces to lose. Also, multiple pieces compromise rod sensitivity. Some rod cases may be soft-sided nylon jobs with sleeves for each piece of the rod. These take up less room. Those in plastic cases are safer still. We've all seen fly-fishing rod carriers, those long cylinders that protect the precious cargo inside, whether in the car or on a plane trip to Alaska. I find these cylindrical rod carriers a bit bulky for backpacking. And the more casing around a rod, the less you will fish. I err on the side of chance more often than not, strapped to the outside of my pack. But I have seen reel handles come up missing once at camp, mysteriously having fallen off along the trail.

Where are you going? If walking among meadows and open Ponderosa pine forests of the Blue Mountains in eastern Arizona, I will not worry about losing my rod and will bring a two-piece rod. However, if I'm backpacking thickly wooded trails to fish rhododendron-cloaked trout streams in the Appalachians I will certainly consider using a multipiece rod that breaks down to fit inside my pack.

Fly rods generally range from 6 to 15 feet, with 8 feet being the norm. Short rods are more difficult to cast and the longer rods, 10 feet or more, can be too cumbersome—too much wind resistance and weight. Finding the proper rod weight is simply a function of the fish for which you will be casting.

Backcountry Fishing

Ultralight spin-fishing gear is built to be as light as possible yet still be able to handle fish. These ultralight outfits can weigh less than a pound, including rod and reel. Weightwise, this is a boon for backpackers, and it also makes the fishing fun and challenging. I use ultralight tackle while backpack-fishing and fishing by boat whenever possible.

Rod Guides

Guides, also known as eyelets, are the rings placed along the rod through which the fishing line flows. The one closest to the reel is called the lead guide, and the one on the end of the rod is called the tip guide or end tippet. Most guides are metal with an inner ring of ceramic for smoothness. The more expensive the rod, the better the guides.

Rod Handles

Cork handles are the traditional material used here. Cork is smooth on the hands, yet provides gripping power when squeezed on and handles getting wet. Other grips are made of plastic or foam/gel. I prefer cork. Make sure the reel will fit on the rod between the sliding clamps and the reel seat, located just above the handle.

Summary

The size, materials, and components determine rod price. It's worth paying more for a name brand rod. I prefer to stick with brands that have worked for me over the years, including Shimano and Quantum. Mitchell, primarily known for reels, also makes good rods, found in rod–reel combo packages. Finally, the Ugly Stick line of rods by Shakespeare can stand the wear and tear of backcountry fishing. Speaking of rod–reel packages, don't be afraid to go in that direction. The rod and reel are designed to work well together. Excellent combos exist. Just stick with a name brand. The sky is the limit as far as spending money on a fly rod. Before dropping the big bucks make sure you will be willing to take it into the backcountry.

Places to buy fishing equipment range from big-box stores such as Wal-Mart, to fishing franchise stores such as Bass Pro Shops, to specialty fly-fishing shops, to every kind of mom-and-pop store located near fishing destinations. I suggest acquiring gear sooner than later to avoid running into unexpected troubles acquiring a specific rod, lure, or other item.

Backcountry Rod Repair

In the middle of a 14-night backpack-fishing trip in the Smoky Mountains, I hung my lure in brush while angling Eagle Creek. I strongly tugged the rod, trying to dislodge the lure, when the lure suddenly came free. The force of my pull smacked the rod onto a large boulder, breaking the upper part in half. I gasped in shock, but luckily had a small packable rod repair kit back at the campsite. I gloomily slogged to camp, hoping it could be fixed. I first overlapped the two broken ends of rod, then tightly coiled fishing line around the ends, wrapping around and around along two inches of the rod. I then heated rod repair gluestick with a lighter, and dabbed it over the line, effectively gluing the line to the rod. Over all this I wound some white medical tape, produced by some nonfishing backpackers, and thus fixed the rod.

Using my example, you could substitute duct tape for medical tape, but a rod repair kit is essential. This consists of a gluestick and different sized tips that fit the tip-end eyelet of a rod, which is the eyelet most often broken. Even if I hadn't been able to mend my rod together, I could've just attached an end eyelet at the break, then continued using the rod, albeit making it much shorter.

The Reel

Reels have lots of moving parts, and thus are the source of both misery and joy in the backcountry. A good reel helps catch fish and a bad reel can turn a fishing trip into a nightmare. When backcountry fishing, do not scrimp on a reel. What separates good reels from poor ones are the number of ball bearings, which are strategically placed to make the reel innards run more smoothly. The more ball bearings a reel has, the more smoothly it will perform. Good reels will have two stainless steel ball bearings. The more expensive, the more ball bearings the reel will have. The three primary types of reels are spin cast, spinning, and bait cast. Spin cast reels are typically closed faced and use a thumb cast button to release line. These are good for beginners, but have little feel. Bait cast reels can be hard to master. They are most often found in bass angler's boats and are easily the most problematic reels. I suggest using an open-faced spinning reel. They come in all sorts of sizes for the backcountry angler. A spinning reel is easy to cast, can be cast with precision, and it's also easier to remove line tangles.

The old saying is that fly reels are used just to store line. The reels are stationed at the rear underside of the rod and connected to the rod by the reel seat. Another function of the reel is to provide drag for fish runs. Make sure the drag can be completely disengaged from the reel when needed. Match the size of the reel to the size of the rod.

Gear Ratio

This refers to how many times the reel spool goes around per turn of the reel handle, determining how fast line is reeled in. Overall, the lower the ratio, the lesser the reel, though low-ratio rods have their place, especially trolling. Backcountry fishers will want a higher gear ratio for a speedier retrieve.

Drag

I was on the famed Chattooga River that forms the border between Georgia and South Carolina, deep in the mountains. I had spent most of the day hiking along the river, peering into the rapids and pools, imagining where a fish might or might not be. The late afternoon sun was descending behind fall's golden trees. I was anxious to see if my "water ciphering" would prove fruitful. I slipped to the backside of a large pool and cast a rainbow Rapala into the moving water above the pool. Wham! A big 'un hit on the first cast, tugging hard before leaping into the air—a rainbow trout, and at least four pounds. After reaching the apex of his leap, the feisty fish twisted away, popping my line, taking my lure and hopes with him into the depths of the pool. What happened? I checked my drag and found it too tight. There wasn't enough "give" in the line to unwind itself from the spool in the event of a big tug from a large fish. Instead the line had snapped. This often happens with the first fish of the day. And that big one was my first one. Check the drag and set it before you start to fish!

Drag is a sort of "valve" for line to be released from the spool of the reel. When setting the drag, you determine the level of pull that will allow line to come out of the reel. In the above example, my drag was set too tight, forcing the line to snap before building sufficient tension to allow the line to come out of the reel. If the drag is set too light, then a fish will often make a strong tug on the line, allowing it to come out too quickly, loosening the line enough for the fish to get away. If the drag is set just right, then a fish will pull line from the reel while neither snapping the line nor overly loosening the line.

I test my drag with a simple pull, then loosen or tighten the dial at the front of the reel, giving a pull approximate to the backcountry fish being sought, whether it's a small brook trout in Appalachian headwaters or a big ol' snook in the Everglades. The proper way to test drag is to bend the rod and pull your line from the last eyelet, the tip eyelet. No matter how accurately the drag is set, the best laid plans can blow up. Say you are fishing for bream in the lower Wisconsin River and a northern pike takes the lure. The line will peel off the reel as if it was shot from a cannon. Consider adjusting the drag while the fish is on the line, tightening it a bit in this case. Other times, if a big fish is on the line, I may loosen the drag early in the fight, preventing line snap, but tighten it when the fish is worn down. But be careful, as fighters may have a few more runs in them when nearing the boat or shore. While fishing, occasionally check your drag to make sure it is set where you deem appropriate.

Spool

A spool is the round device where the line is spun in the reel. Many reels come with interchangeable spools, enabling rapid changing out lines of differing test. Spools are usually aluminum or graphite. Aluminum spools are more durable. Any spool that comes with a reel is designed to hold an adequate amount of line designed for that reel and will be stated on the reel. For example, an ultralight spinning rod is going to hold 100 or more yards of four-pound-or-less test line.

Bail

This is the wire mechanism outside the main reel body that either prevents or allows line to come off the spool. Cast with the bail open and reel with the bail closed. Make sure the bail is completely open before you cast and completely closed before reeling. Some open-faced reels come with a built-in bail trigger. I find they don't always flip the bail open and are in the way, especially after having become proficient with an open-faced reel already. Stay away from them.

Handle

The handle is used to turn the innards to reel in the line. Some open-faced reels have interchangeable handles. This way, the angler can reel either right- or left-handed. Make sure the interchangeable handle is tightly screwed onto the reel before fishing.

Summary

When purchasing a reel, consider reel size, not only for the quarry, but also with which rod it will be used. The more ball bearings the better. Higher gear ratio is important when it comes to precisely reeling in lures. Usually good reels have good parts throughout. Again, you get what you pay for.

Reel Maintenance

A well-oiled reel will prevent problems in the backcountry. Consider bringing a small vial of reel oil that weighs next to nothing. I recommend Reel Magic by Blakemore. It's odorless when dry and really helps reel performance. Also check all the screws and make sure everything is screwed in together, especially the handle. Wash a reel used in salt water. Check the bail alignment. If the bail is bent it will not operate correctly. Gently and carefully bend the bail back into place.

Reels in the Backcountry

While you're backcountry in a canoe, and especially a kayak, the reel will get wet, whether it's from a rainstorm filling the bottom of the boat, an errant wave rolling over the kayak, or sticking the rod in too deep while trying to dislodge a hung lure. If wetted in freshwater, immediately cast the line out and reel it in a few times. This will get rid of the excess water. Same goes if the rod was out during an overnight rain. A well-oiled rod won't suffer, but there is no need to leave excess water in the reel. Salt water can be brutal on a reel. If a rod is dunked, it is very important to cast the line several times. Consider hitting it with lubricant immediately. And if there is any freshwater to spare, rinse out the reel. Consider yourself lucky if the reel is rained on, but crank it out a few times to work the freshwater through the gears. Always rinse out a reel with freshwater when returning from any saltwater backcountry trip. Furthermore, rinse out the boat and just about everything else with freshwater.

Before You Leave

A quick gear check at home will save a lot of misery later. If you find a problem, fix it on the spot or stop at a store en route to the backcountry fishing destination. The farther you are going for a trip, the more prepared you should be. After all, if spending big bucks to fly-fish Montana, why not take the time to be prepared? Having no stores in the backcountry is what makes it backcountry. Check your line Is it brittle? A new trip can mean new line. Is there some spare line in your kit? Check the rod tippets. Did the end get smashed while on the way home from the last trip? Carry a tippet repair kit. Practice reeling. Is it smooth? Or could it use a touch of oil? Now, go over the flies/lures. Do you have enough of what is needed? If a brown floating crawfish brought in the bass on the last trip down Black Creek of Mississippi, make sure to have some this trip.

Fishing Line

Fishing line is the primary connection between you and the fish. And it is also the number one area of failure when the connection between you and the fish is broken. Regard fishing line with as much concern as where to fish, how to fish, and with what to fish.

What Pound Test/Leader?

Way back when, while I was fishing an ultraremote unnamed stream in the Smoky Mountains, dusk approached as I drew near a large pool. I cast the lure toward the head of a pool and thought I was hung when I felt a heavy resistance on the end. Then my line shot out toward the far bank. I had a lunker hooked, and he was running for his life. I slowly worked the fish toward me. My rod bent nearly 90 degrees, its tip twitching with life. A big one was on the line, and I slowly worked it in, edging it toward the bank. The fish was making its way downstream. He was so close—a large, colorful rainbow. I reached to grasp him but he exploded, dashing off again. My line screamed off the reel. I tightened my grip on the rod, keeping a precarious hold. Then all of a sudden—pop! The line had broken.

With shaky hands, I hurriedly put on another lure and cast. Boom! I got another strike right away. I worked him near me. I pulled him out of the water, to flip him onto the bank, desperately wishing I had a net. While getting him out of the water, he twitched and again the blasted line snapped. I was beyond shock. My head swam. My heart pounded. My eyes watered. I stumbled in disbelief at my bad luck.

Earlier, I had purchased two-pound test line, instead of the usual four-pound line. I asked myself, "Have you ever caught a trout over two pounds in the Smokies?" I had not and went ahead with the purchase. What I had not reckoned with was the tenacious nature of these mountain fish. Their strenuous resistance to being reeled in combined with the added strain of fast moving water accounted for the extra tension put on the puny two-pound line. I have since caught trout over two pounds in the Smokies but have never used two-pound line again—anywhere.

When considering line test, think about the type of fish as well as the fishing locale. Also, what reel to use—reels usually have information on them as to what pound test line to use and the optimum number of yards to be used. When backcountry fishing, match the line to the fish, and no more. I tend to go under if anything, despite the above story. Generally speaking, backcountry anglers aren't going to be muscling largemouth bass out from a weed bed. The lighter the line, the farther and more precise casts can be made. However, weigh this against losing lures. Fish will often run for cover when hooked, heading to submerged logs, limbs and the like, leaving you unable to muscle them away with lighter line. The expense and frustration of losing lures (and the fish lost with them) add up. Have plenty of backup line, in case of tangles, tree casts, or other means of losing line. By all means, do everything reasonable to retrieve lost line. Stray line is bad for nature's beasts, and nobody likes seeing line hanging over the water.

What Style of Line?

Nowadays, line comes in more types than you can be imagine. Consider not only line test, but thickness, color, and other line variations, such as "smooth casting" or "tough." Back in the bad old days, fishing line was made of horsehair or catgut. We've come a long way, baby: most line today is oil-based, made of nylon, Dacron, and so on. Spools most often come as monofilament—a single strand of line. Fluorocarbon lines are two materials fused together. Yet other lines are braided, such as Spiderwire, which uses gel-spun polyethylene fibers.

Fly lines have a core that is wrapped in a plastic sheath imbedded with tiny air bubbles to give buoyancy and reduce wear. Fly lines are often tapered monofilament or fluorocarbon line. The leader is sized in X's, which correspond to its final tip section. The higher the X number of line, such as 6X versus 2X, the smaller the diameter of the line. The end of this leader is called the tippet and is what the fly is tied onto. Leader needs to be thin and strong, yet allow for a natural drift in the water, not to spook the fish.

When freshwater spin-fishing in the backcountry, I generally use four-pound test line. This is strong enough to handle most backcountry fish, such as trout, smallmouth bass, and panfish, but light enough for precision casting, such as is required for small streams and rivers, typical of backcountry destinations. Also, this line will allow long casts, which are preferred while on Western alpine lakes.

Higher test lines will be needed for northern pike and trolling for lake trout in the North Country. In the saltwater backcountry such as North Carolina's Cape Lookout National Seashore, I prefer ten-pound test. I know no matter the test line, there will be some big hits from huge fish, such as sharks, that no fishing line a backcountry angler would have can handle. As far as the varieties of line offered, whether they are "tough," "extra- thin," or "knot-tying," I stick with the smooth casting, though I do wonder the actual difference (I have a notion that some fishing products

When fishing salt water such as the Everglades, make sure your line is strong enough to handle the toothy fish found there.

are marketed for the in-store purchase, rather than performance on the water). I try to match the color of the line with the color of the water. As far as brands go, I was once a Stren loyalist, but now mainly use Berkley Trilene XL Smooth Casting.

Leader

Leader is a short stretch of line tied to the lure on one end and the primary fishing line on the other end. Leaders for fly-fishing and spin-fishing are two different animals. Leader keeps toothy fish from cutting through the line after they are hooked. Otherwise you lose the fish and lure, while the quarry has to wear some lip jewelry for a few days. Leader is essential when fly-fishing. It connects the thicker monofilament to the tapered line to which a fly is tied. Spin-fishing leader is thicker and a higher pound test than the primary line, or the line to which it is attached.

Leader can also be metal. Pike can and will tear through average fishing line like an axe through a twig. While fishing for pike, and using a large spoon, a metal leader between the lure and the line will save some lures, but can dissuade some fish from taking the bait. I prefer the pre-made metal leaders about eight inches in length. Often, while fishing for

Toothy pike are exciting to catch but tough on fishing line and leader.

smallmouth bass in the Boundary Waters, pike will go for a lure intended for bass, and lures are lost. Therefore, a good strategy is to use a leader made of 14- to 17-pound monofilament fishing line between the lure and the main line. Pike will eventually tear through this, but you will save some hardware. In saltwater backcountry areas, such as Texas's Padre Island National Seashore, some seriously big fish, armed with grins resembling paper shredders, will tear through any line a backcountry angler will have. However, fish such as sea trout or mangrove snapper will shy away from a lure tied to a metal leader. Therefore, the same higher test line connected to the main fishing line will help. Otherwise, I do not use metal leaders.

If concerned about losing lures—and who isn't—consider retying the lure after you have caught many fish in a short period or have fished waters with rough bottoms, such as oyster bars or sharp rocks, or a lot of timber. Run a finger up the line starting at the lure to about two feet up the line, feeling for frays. Fishing line is only as strong as its weakest link. If the line is frayed, retie the lure above the fray. I'll be the first to admit that when in the midst of a flurry it can be almost impossible to stop and retie. I also know losing a lure in the midst of a flurry (especially when it's the only one of its type) has made me wish I retied before losing the lure, because after losing the lure due to frayed line I had to stop and retie anyway, minus the lure. Also, many anglers advocate changing an entire spool of line to keep it fresh. They believe that fresh line breaks less often. And we anglers are a superstitious lot by nature, so change line if you think it'll help. And keep that rabbit's foot in your pocket, too. Remember, never throw away line into the environment. Many boat launches have fishing line recycling containers. If you don't want to carry used line around in the backcountry at least burn it.

Line Twist

Often, while trolling with lures or using spinners that go 'round and 'round, you will eventually suffer from line twist. The line will roll into unwieldy curls when it goes slack or twist around an eyelet. When attempting to become unhung, do not pull line so tight that it forces the drag to open up. This will also result in line twist. The only cure is to change line. New line has less "memory" than old line. If fishing with spinners over a long period, line twist will occur as well. Change the line. Make sure to bring extra line, especially while out on a multiday excursion. If you don't have extra line, try this: strip off your line nearly to the end, letting it drift freely—sans lure—behind you downstream or from the boat. After a few minutes, reel in the now less twisted line.

How to Spool a Spinning Reel

First, use the test line recommended for that reel as to poundage and number of yards the spool can handle. Correctly spooling line on a spinning reel will avoid line twist. Respool with fresh line. First, pull off all the old line. Run the line from the new line spool through the rod eyelets to the reel spool. Tie the new line around the reel spool, clipping off any excess line from the knot. Lay the spool of new line on the ground so that

A Note about Line Tangles

Tangle Causes	Tangle Cures
1. Line is twisted from the lure	Change line when twisted from lure
2. Line is not tight against the spool	Reel more smoothly
3. Line is incorrectly spooled	Respool your line correctly

the line comes off spool just as it goes on the reel spool. Hold line tightly with your nonreeling hand just above reel, allowing it to run between your fingers while slowly reeling in the line, making sure it's spooled tightly. Don't fill the whole spool or tangles may ensue.

Knots

Backcountry anglers need to know at least two knots among the boatload that are out there: the improved clinch knot and the double surgeon's knot. Fly-fishers need to know more knots. Some anglers like to wet the lines before they tie them, believing that it results in a stronger, sturdier knot that's less likely to come apart. The improved clinch knot is used to tie lures directly to the primary fishing line. The knot is easy to tie yet it reduces line strength only slightly.

Improved Clinch Knot

Step one: Run the end of the line through the eye of the lure, and then make at least five turns (I use eight) around the standing part of the line. Run the end of the line through the opening between the eye of the lure and the beginning of the twists, and then run it through the large loop formed by the previous step.

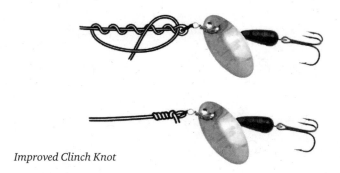

Improved Clinch Knot

Step two: Pull slowly on the standing part of the line, being careful that the end doesn't slip back through the large loop up and that the knot snugs up against the eye. Clip off the excess.

Double Surgeon's Knot

This is used to join two strands of greatly unequal line diameters, say when tying a heavier leader to lighter mainline, or vice versa.

Double Surgeon's Knot

Step one: Place the two lines parallel with the ends facing opposite directions. Using the two lines as a single strand, make a simple overhand knot pulling the two strands all the way through the loop and then make another overhand knot.

Step two: Holding both strands at each end pull the knot tight and clip off the ends.

Fishing Hardware

The following is a list of fishing paraphernalia that will improve fishing and save hassles—from wrangling with gear, to handling fish, to cleaning fish, and more.

Clippers

Simple fingernail clippers are an invaluable aid in making fast lure changes. If you have a lure that you want off your line, simply clip the line and the knot from the lure itself, and properly dispose of the line with the rest of your trash. Feel the line with your finger, and then make sure to cut the line above where it may have been stressed or frayed from being pulled over rocks, hung around itself, or frayed from the business end of a fish. This way, the next lure will be tied with strong and nontwisted line. Then after tying on the next lure, closely trim the excess line from the knot with the clippers, making the lure ready for presentation.

Knife

I don't use a knife as much as others do. Some people trim their line with them. A knife will work in a pinch. Knives are important for other backcountry chores. Bring one along so you won't use your fillet knife to cut rope. Swiss Army knives and multitools come in handy in the backcountry, whether you are pulling a splinter from your foot with tweezers or opening a can.

Fillet Knife

A fillet knife is another matter. A fillet knife is a must if you plan to keep and cook your catch. Make sure it's sharp. I still remember with regret the four-pound smallmouth I mangled with a dull fillet knife on the Buffalo River of Tennessee. It was about dark when we pulled up to camp. It had been a while since my friend had been fishing, and he failed to check or sharpen his fillet knife before we embarked. I failed to bring my own. His knife was dull. If I had known how little meat would be left after mangling the fish, I would've sent it back to fight another day. When purchasing a fillet knife, make sure it is sharp and it has a sturdy sheath. (My brother cut his hand on a fillet knife when it went straight through the leather sheath he'd put it in.) Most blades today have a locking blade and snapping sheath, because a sharp fillet knife will cut anything on contact. Don't play around with a fillet knife and don't use it for anything other than cleaning fish. Consider bringing a whetstone to keep it sharp, especially on a multiday trip.

Hemostats and Pliers

Hemostats are used to separate your lure from the fish. For years I was a fan of average hospital-type hemostats. They sure worked better than sticking your fingers in a fish's mouth trying to extract the lure. Especially after that last time I went without hemostats on a trout/bass stream near home. I caught so many fish my fingers were pricked from unhooking a two-treble hooked floating Rapala. (It was one of those days that you never forget. That is why we love fishing. We tend to forget the fishless days and remember those days when we slayed them—but we also seem to remember the big ones that got away just as clearly.) But the last straw was when a feisty trout fought back. The front treble was still in the fish's mouth, and when he vigorously shook, a hook on the back treble went into the meat of my finger then back out the other side. I unhooked the fish from the lure and considered the dilemma. The barb was all the way through my finger so I couldn't just push it back. And because it was a treble hook I couldn't pull it through. I tried to cut the hook out, but found it's hard to operate on yourself. So I got the hook off the lure and commenced to paddling down the river until I ran into some other anglers. Luckily, one man had a pair of pliers. As rusty as they were I sure was glad to see them, after running through some fairly mean rapids with a treble hook in my hand. I cut the hook off and pulled it on through. Lesson learned.

Hemostats are good, but pliers—especially needle-nose pliers—are best. Pliers deliver more torque to get the hook out of a fish, and the wire-cutting edge below the gripping part of the pliers can cut off an embedded hook. Plus, pliers can handle bigger fish, such as those toothy specimens in the saltwater backcountry, and big ol' pike from South Dakota's Big Sioux River. Needle-nose pliers are the best choice, because they are easy to handle.

On the other hand, if you're going for panfish on Econfina Creek in Florida, or seeking brook trout in Virginia's Shenandoah National Park, odds are you won't be unhooking anything of size, therefore a simple pair of hemostats will do. And where weight is an issue, such as while back-packing, standard hemostats are preferred.

Net

I have never been an advocate of nets. It's one more thing to carry along a stream, one more thing to lose while fighting through brush, and I disdain untangling lures from the net. Most fish in backcountry streams can be handled without a net, except of course that once-in-a-lifetime monster. However, consider using a net if trying to land big fish from a canoe or kayak. Once, while in the Everglades, I was in the process of landing a sea trout hooked by the bow paddler from my position in the back of the canoe. She was working the fish toward me and I was about to stick my hand in the water to scoop up the 20-inch sea trout, when a shark shot from behind the boat, surfaced with a pop, engulfed the sea trout and the plug and was gone. I sat in stunned amazement, quaking at the thought of my hand being in the water when the shark struck. Other large toothy fish, such as pike, could be candidates for a net, as would some big Alaskan species, such as King salmon.

Fish Scale

Also known as a de-liar, fish scales come in conventional and electric models that are light enough to take in the boating backcountry and perhaps the hiking backcountry if traveling with an angler known to tell tall fish tales. These verify the weight of the fish and keep the stories respectable around the nighttime campfire. It seems many rod tossers like to estimate their fish on the heavy side. The fish scale doesn't have a dog in the hunt, therefore will accurately determine if you or Uncle Fred caught the biggest of the backcountry adventure.

Ruler/Measurement Device

This is actually more important than a fish scale, since most state creel limits use inch measurements when determining a keeper from a nonkeeper. Many coolers and creels have a built-in ruler on them. If yours doesn't, then carry a tape measure. A canoe of mine has a water-proof paper ruler with adhesive backing pasted on a thwart, courtesy of the Missouri Department of Natural Resources. If you plan on keeping your fish and size limits are an issue, have a means of measuring the fish. It's better to be safe than sorry. Conservation departments set up size and creel limits to protect resources so that we can all successfully fish in the outback.

How to Measure Fish Length

Total length is measured from the tip of the snout to the end of the tail with the fish laid flat, mouth closed and tail lobes pressed together. With certain parties, in a friendly angling contest, fish will have to be remeasured in person, especially if they are your brothers.

Lure Retriever

At one time or another, we've all swam for a lure, either because it was working so well or we were so broke we couldn't afford to lose it. A gadget some anglers have is a lure retriever. They come in several varieties. One type hooks on the line and slides down in around the lure. The fisher operates a line attached to the lure retriever, theoretically getting it unstuck. Others are heavier weights that slide down the line and knock the lure. Some people use a pole retriever, a collapsible aluminum pole with a hook, coil, or plug knocker on the end. These not only work under water but also get lures out of trees—not that you or I would ever throw a lure into a tree.

Fish Scaler

Bring this along if planning to cook whole fish. Many cold-water species such as trout and char don't need scaling, but panfish and bass do if they are to be cooked with the skin on. Scalers are more efficient than using a spoon.

Choosing the right lure at the right time in the right place is key to successful backcountry angling.

Anchor

Anchors are good for river trips with no portaging required. They come in handy if wanting to fish moving water without moving the boat. However, they do weigh down the boat. Rather than bring an anchor, I try to find an eddy to fish from, or get out of the boat and wade-fish, if on a river rapid or sweet spot. In portaging country, there is no need to carry a full-fledged anchor. Nowadays, anchors weighing mere ounces, made of plastic straps that resemble a bucket, can be tied to a rope and then to the boat. Simply supply a big rock, set it inside the plastic mesh and an anchor is born. But think before dropping anchor. Once, in trout tailwater on the Chattahoochee River in Georgia, my friend had anchored his canoe below Buford Dam. We were having success with trout. The warning sirens of an impending dam release and my strong suggestions could not dissuade him from pulling up anchor. The water release came and soon engulfed the canoe, tipping us over and sending us downstream. We lost everything, including the canoe, the fishing tackle and my wallet.

The Lures

Hunting fish with lures is an exciting element of backcountry fishing. Plus there is an added skill level needed to fool a fish with artificial bait.

You choose the lure that you think will cause the fish to strike. Walk into mega-sized fishing store and the sheer number and variety of lures available today can overwhelm you. So where do you start? My advice is to keep it simple. Find something that works and stick with it. Don't try to get too smart with some ultrafancy untested lure. Some tried and true lures work in most waters. That being said, investigate as many sources as possible prior to your trip—Internet, guides, outfitters, as well as game and fish officers.

Plugs. Plugs generally try to mimic minnows, though others can imitate crawfish, frogs, and more. The action of plugs is what backcountry anglers bank on, whether it is the water noise of a surface popper or the wiggles of a shallow diver. Plug choice is first determined by the type of fish you're going after. You must then consider three main factors: plug type, size, and weight. Say I am kayak fishing on North Carolina's Fontana Lake. I am going topwater for smallmouth bass along the shoreline. I will want a surface popper or one that makes some kind of noise. The bass will average in the one- to two-pound range, so I will want a smaller plug yet one that weighs enough to be cast freely. I decide to use a Heddon Tiny Torpedo. It rests on the surface while the propeller creates noise, bringing

Topwater plugs on warm-water rivers can result in exciting catches such as this smallmouth bass.

bass to the surface. I normally try to stick to natural colors, so I'll use a green one with the white underbelly. With all lures remember the adages: "dark day, dark lure, bright day, bright lure," and "the colder the water, the slower the retrieve." I also like to match the water color. In brown waters I am more apt to use a brown/gold lure, whereas in green waters I will be more likely to try silver.

Popping plugs have a concave front. When retrieving the lure in a jerking fashion, the concave face pops, splashes, and makes noise. Shallow runners generally stay a foot or two below the surface. They will often have an attached lip that makes them wobble back and forth on the retrieve. This wobbling is designed to catch the eye of the fish with both movement and the lure reflecting light, much like a disco ball. Floater-diver plugs combine the actions of a topwater plugs with those of shallow runners. I prefer these because they give me an opportunity get a top-water hit, yet I can still catch fish on the retrieve. Sinking plugs do what you would imagine; you have to reel them at a consistent speed to maintain a consistent depth and to keep from being hung on the bottom. Deep diving plugs have very large lips. When retrieved these large lips force a plug to go deep down, wobbling as they go. For backcountry fishing I have had the most success with surface plugs and floater-divers. While using surface plugs, whether they are poppers or those with propellers—no matter the disturbance they create—catching fish on topwater offers unparalleled excitement. Backcountry fishing waters tend to be shallow, which is why I stick with plugs that stay at or near the surface.

Spinners. Spinners are among the most versatile lures for the freshwater backcountry angler. They work on small Appalachian creeks, bigger touring rivers, and lakes from the Adirondacks to the Sierras. Designed to imitate baitfish, spinners attract our finned friends by flash and vibration. If I had three lures only for the rest of my life, one of them would be a spinner. Spinners come in various sizes, from tiny 1/32-ounce models to those weighing 1/2 ounce and even heavier. A blade, most often in gold or silver, is attached to a body of various colors. A single hook or treble hook is attached to the lower end. The hooks can be dressed or undressed, that is, have material disguising the tail hook and adding more color and action to attract the fish, perhaps trying to mimic something the fish would long for. I prefer to stick with silver and gold models for two reasons: they work, and you can see them in the water. It is fun to follow the lure and watch it get struck. Based on my experience, Panther Martins are the best, most consistent spinner.

27

Spoons. These are the granddaddies of all artificial lures. The story goes like this: A man accidentally dropped a spoon in the water of a lake and watched as the fish went for it while the spoon fluttered to the lake bottom; thus, the spoon as a lure was born. Spoons also imitate baitfish, attracting them with flash and movement. They have either a single fixed hook, often weedless, or a freely moving treble hook. (A weedless hook uses a bendable shaft of metal extending from the top of the lure to nearly connect to the tip of the hook, keeping weeds from becoming caught on the curve of the hook. However, the shaft will bend easily when a fish bites the lure and thus can become hooked). Backcountry fishers will most often use spoons in deeper lakes. They don't perform as well in shallower moving water, being more difficult to precisely control them on the reel. They also tend to be hooked at the bottom of shallow water. That being said, spoons have their place.

Jigs. A jig is a lure with a lead head on one end and a fixed hook on the other, and anything from rubber to feathers to fur in the middle. The decorative variations can extend from head to tail. Jigs are most commonly thought of as having a replaceable rubber body, and are popular for use in salt- and freshwater. Backcountry anglers often use them when going after walleye. Rubber worms may be considered a subset of the jig kingdom.

Making Lures Barbless

In Great Smoky Mountains National Park, my trout-fishing training ground, only single-hook artificial lures are allowed, applying to both fly- and spin-fishers. On the way to the park, while stocking up with lures, we would find a favorite of the long-ago days, such as an orange Roostertail spinner, which was colored to mimic the many crawfish found in the streams. Sometimes we could find single-hook models, and other times we couldn't. The orange Roostertail might be there, but the lure had a treble hook at its base, which just weren't legal. We would fish them anyway, practicing our pleadings of innocence. I mentioned this problem to an old-timer we met on Forney Creek, while camping on the North Carolina side of the Smokies. He made my lures legal on the spot, pulling pliers from his overalls, snipping two barbs off my spinner, and presto, my lure was now legal. Today, many trout streams, such as the Bogachiel River of Washington's Cascades National Park, go one step further, being single-hook barbless streams, as in barbless hooks. The pliers will work here, too—just crimp down the barb, but do a good job and do it right. Backcountry anglers are not above playing by the rules. Barbless streams are almost always catch-and-release, and the more lightly hooked, the higher the survival rate of the released fish. When backpack backcountry fishing, pliers can be a bit weighty, so do your metal work at home, or keep a pair of pliers in your vehicle and fix your lures before hitting the trail. This can apply to treble hook lures or multiple treble hooked lures used in saltwater outback, especially when practicing catch and release. No matter where you do it, dispose of the cut hooks where they won't stick someone. I've been stuck while traipsing barefoot at a backcountry campsite on a trout stream. If you are catch-and-release sportfishing, single-hook barbless presents a greater challenge, and it puts more sport into the fishing!

Most often associated with largemouth-bass fishing in backcountry situations, rubber worms are generally used in slow-moving rivers of the Deep South.

Backcountry Tackle Boxes

Anglers heading into the outback by foot should keep their tackle box small and of packable size. I'm talking stick-in-your-pocket-or-vest small. Most of these boxes are plastic, open on both sides, and are no larger than two or three decks of cards. They will hold enough flies and or spinners to get you through a day trip as well as a backcountry overnight trip.

Boaters' Tackle Box

Backcountry boaters can get away with a larger tackle box and more tackle. I recommend one no bigger than a bread box, simply because there is limited room, whether you are floating a river or portaging lakes. Kayakers generally have less room and should consider tackle boxes used by backcountry anglers on foot. This can be challenging when trying to whittle down their best saltwater lures, because they are generally bigger than freshwater lures. For kayakers, where to put the tackle box is the biggest problem. It's likely to get splashed if simply strapped to the top of the kayak, there is limited space in the waterproof rubber dry bags used by paddlers, and there simply isn't room in the cockpit for a standard tackle box. If you put the box in one of the waterproof storage hatches in the boat, it's impossible to get into without pulling over and getting out of the boat. I go with a smaller tackle box that can stow away in my deck dry bag.

Keep all your fishing gear together in your tackle box—you always know where to go for quick access, whether it is lures, a line, pliers, fingernail clippers or other hardware. No matter the size, keep your tackle box dry. When a tackle box gets wet, lures get wet and rust, becoming less usable and wasting your investment. Also, tackle boxes sometimes become storage boxes for other stuff. I have seen rusty knives, pliers and other metal items rendered worthless after wetting. Water almost always accumulates at the bottom of a boat; therefore a standard box with a top-lifting lid is best for boaters. It keeps water out. Pocket-sized dual-opening tackle boxes are a poor choice for canoeists. They are prone to get wet on the side lying on the canoe bottom.

Speaking of tackle boxes, have you ever been floating in a canoe on a sun-drenched afternoon that was passing as slowly as the fish are biting? It's so hot and still that even the bugs aren't moving. Then suddenly you hear the snap of a tackle box followed by the light clinking of lures as your fishing partner desperately searches for something that will work. You snicker to yourself, knowing the opening of the box is an admission of lure failure.

Completely shut your tackle box between uses. I have picked up a tackle box by the handle only to see my hardware spill onto the boat, right when I am eager to change lures after spotting a reason to change a lure—namely my fishing partner catching a fish on a different lure than I am using. I am shameless when it comes to changing lures to what is working. If portaging, keep your tackle box of reasonable size, because this is one more thing to carry. I usually carry my rod in hand and strap my tackle box onto the portage pack.

Anglers on foot often will use a fishing vest simply because it's high enough off the water to keep their box and other stuff dry. While back-country wade-fishing, I normally don't intentionally end up in stomach-deep waters with a box in my pants pocket; I just start trying to work around a fallen tree or take one step too many into the deep water, trying to get lined up for that perfect cast. Keeping your tackle box in a vest eliminates that problem, and is a great choice fishing for the day. If going overnight in the backcountry you have to commit to carrying a fishing vest the entire trip, which is added weight. And as stated before and cannot be stated too often, backcountry fishing is limited by space and weight. Making good choices concerning space and weight separates successful from unsuccessful backcountry anglers.

Live Bait

Live bait is difficult to carry around with you in the backcountry. Furthermore, many backcountry areas prohibit the introduction and use of live bait, because nonnative species are introduced into the natural ecosystem. While boating, live bait can be more practical for the first day or two out. The best situations for backcountry bait-fishing is from camp, when you can dig up some worms or find other bait yourself, and then tight line fish in deep holes. This way you don't have to tote the bait around and aren't introducing exotic minnows or other creatures into the ecosystem.

The primary types of easily purchased freshwater bait are worms, crickets, and minnows. These are usually fished two ways—either by tight-lining, suspending with weights and being carried by the current or sunk to the bottom with hooks above the weight, or suspended to a bobber floating at the surface with hooks below the weight. Just about anything will go after live bait, which is the exciting part of bait-fishing. However, bait-fishing is more of a sit-and-wait proposition, rather than hunting fish with lures. Furthermore, bait has a limited shelf life. Heat and sun are the two biggest enemies of live bait. Keep your bait cool and in the shade if possible.

Casting, or Where Do I Throw My Line?

Casting While on Your Feet

I was working my way up Big Wilson Creek at Virginia's Mount Rogers National Recreation Area, climbing falls between deep, green pools when I came upon an exquisite hole. Water crashed clear and cold down a rock face and tapered into a yawning pool, where the water slowed into a perfect holding situation for the brown trout that lurked there. Mountain laurel and rhododendron canopied the entire pool, including from where I would have cast. Even with my four-and-a-half-foot rod, I couldn't get a throwing angle to get the lure to the back of the hole. I called up a casting trick I had learned way back when—the ol' bow and arrow cast. I opened the reel bail, let out a few feet of line, carefully grabbed the lure, pulled back the line, bending the rod backward, then let go of the lure and let it fly, propelling the lure forward between the thickets into the back of the pool, and reeled in as usual. I didn't catch a fish that cast but I got the lure in position to catch a fish. (Sometimes, when you make the perfect cast and the fish doesn't strike—it's the fish's fault!)

Backcountry fishing by foot, namely stream-fishing, will inherently have all sorts of obstacles to overcome and situations to handle in order to get to the fish. However, before you cast, make sure you are securely positioned, whether you're in the water or on the bank. Secure footing will result not only in a better cast, but it will keep you from slipping and sliding as you cast, potentially ruining the fishing hole.

Types of Casts

To catch fish, you will need all the casts you can conjure up, including the bow and arrow cast. Under ideal conditions, use the simple forward cast. First, open the bail of the reel, hold the line with your finger, cock your arm back, and let her fly. Watch out for high limbs overhead—they're often overlooked when the main stream seems open. Use the sidearm cast when the trees are a little too thick overhead. Keep your rod low and arm open to the direction toward which you want to throw, then let the lure go *before* ❯

your rod is pointing directly at your target. Your follow-through will carry the lure to its intended target. You can also lob your lure with an upward sidearm cast for a gentler landing. Start with your rod tip low and shift upward as you make the sidearm throw. The backhand cast is much like the backhand stroke in tennis. This is also used when there is neither room overhead nor room for you to cast on the side of your throwing arm. Because you have the rod backed up to your chest, there isn't much room to sling the rod, so you have to use more of a quick flick motion to propel the lure forward. For a backhand lob, keep your rod tip low and flip it upward, much like tennis again.

About Wading

Backcountry anglers will often be casting while in the water. Knowing how to safely wade a stream is important. For starters having felt-soled shoes makes stream life a lot easier and safer. That said, a swift current can quickly sweep you off your feet. Therefore, never take a step in any direction, upstream or downstream, unless one foot is firmly planted. Once one foot is planted you can slide your other foot forward until you feel something secure below you, whether it be gravel, a rock crevice, or some type of vegetation that may hold better than a flat, slick rock. Once your front foot is in a secure spot, slide your rear foot forward. Be careful when lifting your feet off the streambed while under the water. You must factor in the current flow when planting a lifted foot. Before proceeding, always look ahead upstream to see where you are going, avoiding routes that are too deep or lead into a nearly vertical wet slick bluff, log pile, or other obstacle. Also, consider getting out and walking along the bank, avoiding particularly swift waters or slick streambed. If you do lose your balance, lower your fishing rod into the water. The rod buoyancy and its hitting the water may be enough to keep you from taking a full spill. If you do fall, brace yourself for a potential cold-water jolt, but don't panic. If the water is deep enough to force you to float, float facing *downstream* on your back with your feet at the water surface to keep your legs from getting stuck between rocks, and then use your arms to swim to shallower water.

A wading staff is the answer for some. The best of these is the Folstaf, an ingenious collapsible wading staff that folds up and attaches to your belt when not in use. Then after reaching your destination you can unfold the staff and use it in the river. When not in use the staff simply floats in the water and stays attached to you by a cord.

Casting from a Boat

Casting lures from inside a boat is a different proposition than casting from the land. For starters, you are sitting down or should be sitting down rather than standing. Instead of being perfectly still while casting, your boat is moving while you're trying to aim for the intended target, whether it be an eddy on the downstream side of a rock or a root system against the shoreline. Not only is the canoe moving, but it's moving at varying speeds and directions. Therefore you must be able to adjust your casts on the fly—and watch around you, as well as look for fish.

Two of us were paddling the Yellow River in south Alabama. The temperatures were quite cold, and we were heavily clad. We passed an area with particularly inviting deep holes, so both of us were fishing hard. We didn't pay attention to the boat, which had drifted perpendicular to the fast current. Before you could say "largemouth bass" we hit a submerged log and went headlong into the water, soaking our gear and ourselves. We immediately recovered everything, climbed into the pines and made a rip-roaring fire to dry off our clothes and ourselves, deciding to camp there for the night, since our fishing was over for the day. Pay attention to where the boat is going lest you bounce into a rock or log and go sideways down a rapid. Don't assume the other person in the boat is paying attention to where you are going or you will end up as we did—in the drink. This is the responsibility of everyone in the boat.

Depending upon the river size and situation, you may be float-fishing along one bank of the river for an extended period of time. Say you are floating down a river and for whatever reason the left bank is more promising. You will be casting to the left almost exclusively that entire time, so whether you're right-handed or left-handed you'll have to adjust your cast while repeatedly throwing to the left. A right-handed person will have no problems, but a lefty like me will be switching back and forth between shifting my shoulders to face the shoreline and using a simple forward cast, or keeping my shoulders facing the front of the boat and using a backhanded cast. Contorting your body to properly place your shoulders aids casting accuracy. Ask anybody who has executed a multi-night backcountry paddle-fishing trip and they will reveal what the contorting does to their neck. But the fish are worth it.

When fishing from a boat, you will use all the previously mentioned casts, but there is one other factor that generally doesn't come in to play when backcountry fishing by foot, and that is wind. Backcountry boat-accessible areas are naturally bigger and have more open bodies of water, which allows more wind to sweep upon your fishing area. When casting, factor in whether the wind is going with you or against you. With the wind at your back you can make extraordinarily long casts. Keep the tip of your rod pointed upward, which will allow the line to really fly. When casting into the wind, keep your rod and your lure low, minimizing your chances of being caught in a gust. You may want to factor wind into the timing of your fishing. In general, winds are calmer in the morning than the afternoon, when winds tend to pick up.

Finally, when backcountry fishing by foot you may have limbs and underwater obstacles upon which to hang. Backcountry boaters have the same obstacles and more, including what's in your boat, such as rubber dry bags, ropes, camping gear, and the other paddler. Be aware as not to hook the wrong thing inside your boat as well as outside your boat.

Becoming Unhung

It was mid-September. Fresh fall winds blew into West Virginia's Cranberry Wilderness. My friend Bryan Delay and I were enjoying some autumn backpack-fishing on the South Fork Cranberry River. I had gone downstream and he was headed upstream. The fall afternoon turned into evening and I returned to camp to find Bryan lying on his back with

Accidents do happen in the backcountry.

a camp mirror in his hand. Something was terribly awry. I came closer and Bryan moved the camp mirror, revealing the rainbow Rapala hooked to his eyelid. Bryan calmly asked me to remove the hooks. I began to do just that when reddish fluids oozed from his eye. At that point a visit to the emergency room was in order. We packed our gear and walked in beyond dark five miles back to the car, whereupon I drove Bryan to the hospital. Along the way he told me his story. He had been casting the plug into a large pool. It hung on some rhododendron, and he had simply jerked the lure to release it. When it released the lure came at him like a missile, smashing into his eye, despite his wearing a ball cap. He never knew what happened. Luckily the lure hooked only into his eyelid. The emergency-room doctor removed it, but his eye was swollen for weeks. To this day, Bryan always wears sunglasses while fishing.

Even the best of us will get hung sometimes, especially when we are aggressively pursuing fish. When hung you do not want to lose your lure. First, gently pull to see if you can release it. After that, extreme jerking will have two results: the line will break, the lure will drop into the water, and you lose it, or the lure will come at you with potentially disastrous results for you or your fishing partner. Think before you act.

Here are some strategies for getting unhung:

Problem	Solution
Hung over a tree limb	Reel line to within a foot or so from a limb and gently flip it over limb
Stuck between rocks under water	Reel line all the way to lure with rod in water, and then push lure
Stuck high in brush or leaves	Jerk downward toward water; if that doesn't work, find long stick or limb to pull limb downward within arm's reach
Stuck in deep hole	Change your position to 180° from where you cast to get stuck and pull
Wrapped around a limb	Go over to limb and unwrap it by hand; no amount of pulling will help
Hooked into life jacket, rope	Use a knife or scissors to cut it out

Backcountry Fishing Excursions

Backcountry Fishing: Day-tripping

So you're going for the day, maybe heading up along the ol' trout stream, to sway a savvy silverback to attack your offering, or perhaps working your way to an alpine lake, or sneak up a crystalline Ozark side stream for bass. No matter your destination, foot-only day trips are the simplest way to go. Keep your gear simple, too. It is all about weight and space. When preparing for a day trip work your way down a list, from fish, to fishing equipment to footwear (See backcountry fishing lists starting on page 174).

After determining the type of fish you will seek, decide which lures/flies will be needed and assemble them in the smallest container possible. Collect the hardware you may need: clippers, hemostats, and so on. Determine the rod to use, and go over it along with the reel to make sure everything is in working order, you have enough line, leader, and so on. Break the rod and reel down, and decide how you will be carrying them into the backcountry, whether in your hand or a rod case. Check the weather and determine what clothing you'll need for the trip. If keeping fish, have a cooler ready to store it. Finally, determine what you'll want or need while on the hike to the fishing destination. These could be necessities such as food and water, a wildflower identification book, or your lucky bandanna from Yellowstone. Assemble the pack, including your fishing footwear. I carry my fishing shoes to the angling spot using a day pack, and then change at the point of fishing. Make sure to have a plastic bag of some sort in which to carry the fishing shoes from your destination back to the trailhead because they'll be wet. Once at the trailhead, double-check to make sure you have everything needed, and then hit the trail.

Upon arriving at the destination I will hide my hiking shoes in the woods along with my pack. Wading is tough enough without toting a bunch of extra stuff. I have never had anybody get my stuff while I was gone fishing. For extra safety, leave the trail and cross to the far side of the waterway you are fishing and stash your stuff. People who would find your stuff over there would have to cross the waterway to do so. The only people likely to do that will be other anglers, who wouldn't mess with your stuff anyway. Most important, enjoy yourself on the water. Our precious spare time is limited and we must make the most of our backcountry fishing experiences.

After returning, consider making notes on the weather, stream conditions, water levels, and your catch. This way you can gather information to determine fishing trends on your favorite streams. This information will help you become a better angler the next time.

Backcountry Fishing: Backpacking

Backpack-fishing brings you the wilderness experience. Your pace changes, your perception changes; you leave the civilized world behind for the natural world, where nature moves at nature's time and space. No phones, cars, or concrete—the great escape. Whether going alone or with others, you will make memories that span beyond fishing. From a pure angling standpoint, backpacking allows increased fishing time. You are in the backcountry day and night, availing yourself more time to fish, simply because you are "living" near a body of water. And camping in the backcountry lends a real feel of the water and the land, to understand its moods, which may help understand the fish there. Backpack-fishing is an inexpensive way to fish somewhere. Backcountry camping is generally free or subject to nominal fees, as opposed to a hotel, lodge, or even a drive-up campground. Yet backpack-fishing has its downside: you have to carry your own food and camping gear for days, in addition to fishing gear. You are subject to the weather 24/7. But when going by foot, you really leave the crowds behind and get to immerse yourself in the outdoors, from sunrise to sunset and beyond, from the streamside environment to the trails and the camps—backcountry fishing in its truest sense. Once settled into the backcountry, it enables you to fish well, especially around dusk and dawn, times when you would ordinarily be heading to or from the fishing hole.

How Far Do I Go and Other Considerations

When planning a backpack-fishing trip, take into account the many other time-consuming activities other than just fishing—hiking, setting up camp, cooking, and general lying around. Make sure to leave some time for fishing. To this end, I try to keep my daily hiking mileages short.

For example, on day one I usually end up at the trailhead later rather than sooner, simply due to drive time and supply runs, and so on. Then I have to pack before finally getting under way. Therefore, day one is going to be short, less than 4 miles. But when I wake up the next morning, I am already in the backcountry, and, if the nearby waters are promising, I will stay at the same campsite two or more nights, eliminating the need to set up/break down camp. However, with two or more fishers, the nearby waters can be exhausted, and we will move on, backpacking to new waters. This way a stream can be thoroughly fished, without having to cover the same waters twice. There are just too many streams to be fished for that!

As far as covering streams, 1 mile per day, depending on the conditions, is a good goal. Now, if you are wading or crawling through a vegetation-choked creek, expect to cover no more than 0.75 miles per day. And if the stream is trail-less, add time getting back downstream. Also, walking downstream can be a dangerous proposition because you're going down falls rather than climbing. Beating your way through the brush is time-consuming and frustrating. You will probably do a combination of stream and bank walking. Allow for plenty of daylight to return to camp. In contrast, an open meadow-bordered stream will be easier to travel and return on, so a mile of stream isn't overly ambitious, and you can blow by less promising waters. Consider the time you will be gone, and make sure to have adequate food, water, and clothing for the time period. I will often go fishing in "sessions." In a stationary camp, I will go on a post-breakfast session, return to camp for lunch, dry my feet and legs for a while, and then go on an afternoon session. I will fish a total of five to six hours per day. Just before dark, I may toss a line nearby the camp, in some likely holes.

My examples may not necessarily be the best times to fish. Consider basing your fishing times on solunar tables. These tables, as the name suggests, are based on the movements of the sun and moon and how they affect wildlife, including fish. Many global-positioning system (GPS) units are equipped with these tables. Just turn on yours, find the Hunt and Fish logo, and let the GPS find your position and deliver the best hunting and fishing times for your given location.

If I'm moving camp, I will hike early, arrive at the next campsite, do necessary camp chores, such as setting up shelter and making food storage precautions, and then go on a short session to feel out the water. I'll then return to camp, strategize, eat, finish the rest of the camp chores, such as gathering wood, and go on a major session, returning before dark.

Backcountry Fishing: By Boat

River, Lake, or Salty Sea?

We were floating the gorgeous Green River through Kentucky's Mammoth Cave National Park. A line of sycamore trees extended beyond the morning river fog. Bluffs rose unseen while mussel-covered gravel bars made faint outlines at the river's edge. A slight chill offset the substantial summer humidity. My brother cast a topwater plug against a log, unleashing a fury-filled bass lure attack. The splash of the fish and the subsequent battle broke the silence and raised our pulses. We felt alive and grateful to be in such a beautiful fishy place.

When fishing backcountry waters by boat, whether traveling with the current or by the strength of your body, you fluidly move on water through eye-pleasing surroundings, floating atop a world where fish swim below. Our country is blessed with backcountry waters aplenty, from slow-moving blackwater streams drifting into the Atlantic coastal plain; spring-bordered waters cutting through rocky canyons; silent ponds lying below towering evergreens; massive lakes with seemingly no shore; and protected coastal areas, where nothing but water, land, and sky extend to the horizon's end. So what's better, a canoe trip to Wisconsin's Sylvania Wilderness, which is primarily still-water lake paddling, or a kayak trip down Florida's Suwannee River, where you let the current do the work? Or do you go to British Columbia's Bowron Lakes Provincial Park, where you stroke your boat on lakes and go with moving waterways?

Consider this: every paddle stroke made is one less moment you can fish. Fewer paddle strokes are generally required for paddling rivers and streams, in contrast to lakes or saltwater destinations. Sometimes, especially when the winds are blowing, open water anglers, such as those on lakes, will have to correct their boat between every cast. Stream paddlers will have to correct as well. The amount of time you'll be able to fish is determined by your position in the canoe. Stern paddlers, those in the back, are relegated to guiding the boat simply because that is where the boat is best steered. The bow paddler can tweak the direction of the boat now and then, but is absolved of steering detail. No matter the waters, the stern paddler always gets more paddle detail. Consider that before you claim your position in the canoe.

Lake paddlers will have to self-propel to get anywhere and will be subject to more wind. However, they have the advantage of being able to embark on a trip, travel somewhere, and then return to the point of

When fishing by canoe, consider getting out and working potentially productive waters.

origin, eliminating a shuttle. Most river travelers start at point A and go downstream, ending at point B. This requires either a car at each endpoint or a shuttle.

How Far Do I Go?

By Canoe. When backcountry fishing by canoe, the preferred fishing and travel distance depends on where you go. When river fishing, you will be partially carried by the current. If all goes well, the bow paddler will paddle little, with the stern paddler steering and paddling some. If you are willing to fish all waters, you will average between 1 and 1.25 miles per hour, depending on current. I have gauged my travel on a GPS many times and while fishing, it seems to end up around this, even including breaks and occasionally paddling over poor waters. I generally try to fish all waters. I like the challenge and sometimes you find fish in good mini-habitats amid otherwise poor waters.

By Kayak. The distance kayak paddlers will cover depends upon whether they are going for the day or going overnight and the kayak they use. Overnight kayakers will generally be in a more streamlined boat that allows them to cover more distance. Kayaks are definitely more efficient than canoes, as far as using the paddler's energy for propulsion. But similarly most kayakers will be the only person in their boat, whereas most canoeists will be going in tandem. That being said, and all else being equal, kayakers will be able to cover more ground than canoeists will.

The Boats

Canoe Types, Features, and Materials

When backcountry fishing by canoe, you will be going on day trips and overnight trips. Overnight trips mean larger loads. When looking for a backcountry fishing canoe, consider potential destinations and the type of water you'll be paddling through. Will it be through still bodies of water or moving rivers? Will you be on big lakes and maybe the ocean, or mild whitewater or sluggish streams? The answer, like my answer, will be a little bit of everything. We want to fish everywhere!

Canoes come in a wide array of oil-based materials and are molded for weight, performance, and durability. Don't waste your time or money with an aluminum canoe for fishing. They're extremely noisy, an attribute that hinders fishing, and are more likely to get hung on underwater obstacles rather than slide over them. When choosing a backcountry fishing canoe, consider material and design. Canoe materials can range from wood to fiberglass to composites such as Polylink 3, Royalex, Kevlar, and even graphite. I prefer more durable canoes with tougher composites, such as Royalex.

Canoe design is comprised of the following factors: length, width, depth, keel, and bottom curve, as well as flare and tumblehome.

Length: Length of a canoe should be at least 16 feet for carrying loads and better tracking. However, good-quality shorter fishing canoes are available. They are often used in ponds, small lakes, and smaller streams for shorter trips.

Width: Wider canoes are more stable and can carry more loads but are slower. Go for somewhere in the middle. Deeper canoes can carry more weight and shed water but they can get heavy. Again, go for the middle ground.

Keel: A keel helps for tracking in lakes, but decreases maneuverability in moving water.

Bottom curve: The more curved the canoe bottom, the less stable the boat. Seek a shallowly arched boat, which is more efficient than a flat-bottom boat, but not as tippy as a deeply curved boat.

Flare: The outward curve of the sides of the boat sheds water from the craft. How much flare you want depends upon how much whitewater you expect to encounter.

Tumblehome: Tumblehome is the inward slope of the upper body of the canoe. A more curved tumblehome allows paddlers to get their paddle into the water easier.

Rocker: The curve of the keel line from bow to stern. More rocker increases maneuverability at the expense of stability. Again, go for the middle ground, unless you're exclusively a lake or flat-water paddler.

And then there are situation-specific canoes, such as whitewater or portaging canoes. Whitewater boats will have heavy rocker and deeper flare, but will be a zigzagging tub on lakes. Portaging canoes are built with extremely light materials and will have a padded portage yoke for toting the boat on your shoulders. Ultralightweight portaging boats can sacrifice durability. So what boat is best for the backcountry angler?

We all can't have a separate canoe for flat-water paddling, whitewater paddling, and small streams or portaging. I recommend multipurpose touring/tripping tandem canoes, those with adequate maneuverability, so you will be able to adjust and react while shooting rapids, or make those quick turns while floating toward a submerged log with rod in hand. You want a boat that can navigate moderate whitewater, can handle loads expected of overnight backcountry anglers, and can track decently through flat-water, so you can fish a lake shoreline instead of constantly steering the boat. If you are solo paddling a tandem canoe, weight the front with gear to make it run true. But if you have a solo boat you can't change it to a two-person boat—the two-person models also allow you to have someone in the boat to whom you can brag after catching the big one.

Consider the Old Town Penobscot 17-foot, long a favorite of mine. It's a great all-around boat that I have used over the years on varied trips, from day paddles on rivers to 100-plus mile Gulf of Mexico treks to surprisingly small streams. Each backcountry angler will be best equipped selecting a canoe to fit a specific purpose. Ultralightweight canoes, such as those built by Wenonah, are designed to be carried from lake to lake via portages. I highly recommend the Wenonah Spirit II 17-foot. At 42 pounds, this ultralight Kevlar boat can perform in the water and not break your back on a portage. This way you can get between fishable lakes more efficiently, minimizing your time on fishless land.

Other times you may be going down rivers with significant stretches of whitewater, where you will want a boat that can take bone-jarring hits from rocks. I suggest getting muted colors that blend with the land and water. All else being equal I prefer a green boat. I can hide it in the brush if necessary, and while on the water fish won't be startled by it floating above them.

About Portaging

Backcountry anglers will sometimes be called upon to portage while getting from one fishing destination to the next. Portaging is the act of carrying your canoe from point A to point B, most often from lake to lake, or around a particularly tough rapid in a river. Kayaks are rarely portaged, simply because an area that requires many portages, such as the Boundary Waters Canoe Area Wilderness in northern Minnesota, canoes are preferred, partly because of their ability to be portaged. Kayaks do not lend themselves to being easily portaged due to their weight and shape.

Portaging involves not only your canoe but transporting your gear as well. Most portages have been used as portages as long as people have been traveling down these waterways; therefore, most portage trails are well established. Portages are measured in rods. A rod is 16.5 feet, the length of an average canoe (320 rods equals 1 mile).

Before trying to carry the canoe and all your gear at once, start with simply carrying the canoe. One of the most difficult parts of a portage is getting the canoe over your head and onto your shoulders in order to be able to carry it. First tip the canoe onto its side with the bottom facing you. Bend down, place your knees under the canoe, grab the thwart, and then raise the boat to your lap. Now, grab the far gunwale and, in one motion, raise the canoe over your head and rest the middle thwart or yoke onto your shoulders, facing toward the front of the canoe. Steady the boat with your arms, and begin walking forward, keeping the front of the canoe lower than the rear, allowing you to see the trail ahead. If getting the canoe over your head is difficult, then consider the two-person lift: Person A stands at the front of an overturned canoe and lifts the front. After the front is lifted, person B walks under the lifted canoe and settles their shoulders onto the thwart and then lifts up to begin carrying the canoe.

Portage Strategies

Some portages closer to put-ins can be busy. Avoid lollygagging and try not to eat lunch or fish from these portages. Sometimes, especially

47

earlier in the year, portage trails can be muddy. Try not to swing around the muddy parts of the trail because it only widens the mud hole. Also, if the bugs are biting, wear long pants and a long-sleeve shirt. Have the bug dope and head net ready. Someone carrying a canoe on top of their head and steadying it with their hands is a great mosquito target.

Some he-men try to carry not only the canoe but also their gear all at once over a portage. The fish may be biting, but who's in that big of a hurry? Besides I don't feel like getting a hernia out in the backcountry. I suggest one person carry the canoe and the second person carry the biggest piece of gear. On short portages, carry all your gear to the other end where you will be once again jumping in the canoe. On longer portages do what is known as staging. Carry the canoe as far as you can. When you begin to tire, look for two closely spaced trees between which you can lean the front tip of the canoe so the boat won't have to be relifted again to resume portaging. Retrieve what gear is left, and carry it to the canoe or beyond. Then backtrack to the canoe and carry it forward. The other person is doing this as well with his or her gear. Be wary about leaving a pack unattended if you have seen bear evidence in the vicinity.

Staging allows you to rest and alternate between walking and carrying the canoe or gear. As far as which person to portage the canoe, we usually just flip a coin and whoever loses does the first portage, then the second person does the next portage and we alternate portages from there on out. This way whoever gets the hard portages is left to the luck of the draw. It'll pretty much even out over the long haul. It's funny, when traveling through Canoe Country, just when you get sick of paddling, here comes a portage. When you get sick of portaging, you can always paddle. But hopefully you'll be fishing more than anything.

Kayak Types and Features

The first consideration in choosing a backcountry fishing kayak is deciding between a sit-on-top model and a sit-in-model, also known as a touring kayak. Sit-on-tops are what their name implies—paddlers sit on top of the boat, whereas a touring kayak requires you to put your body into the boat, leaving your upper half above an enclosed cockpit. Ask yourself, which type of waters are you going to fish? Are you going to fish near shore, on calm flat waters, or are you going to fish bigger waters, such as the islands off Bellingham, Washington, or other oceanic destinations? If fishing bigger water you will need a cockpit. Sit-on-top kayaks are generally more comfortable, and allow for more freedom of movement. They also take on water more readily and are used almost exclusively in warmer-water destinations. Sit-in touring kayaks are inherently more stable because the user sits on the bottom of the boat, rather than on top of the boat. Sit-on-top kayaks make up for this stability shortcoming by being wider, which makes them slower. Base your decision primarily on what types of waters you will be fishing and whether you will be going overnight in your kayak. Sit-on-top kayaks are a poor choice when it comes to overnight camping, thus you are limited in your backcountry fishing options to day fishing only. However, sit-on-tops do have their place. Smaller waters, such as tidal creeks and gentle, smaller streams are good for sit-on-top kayaks.

Sit-in kayaks are the traditional kayaks based on models used by Arctic aboriginals. Some factors to consider when choosing a touring kayak are length, volume, and steering. These touring kayaks are built to cover ground and longer boats track better. Look for a boat anywhere from 14 to 18 feet in length if overnighting. Shorter day-tripping kayaks are a good choice for the backcountry angler.

Sit-on-top kayaks will range generally from 8 to 15 feet. Narrow touring kayaks have less initial stability—they feel more tippy when you get into them, although their narrowness prevents waves from flipping the boat over as waves will tip wider sit-on-top kayaks, which have better initial stability.

Kayak materials vary from the traditional skin-and-wood of the Inuits to plastic and fiberglass composites such as Kevlar and the waterproof cover of folding kayaks. (Folding kayaks have an assembled frame and skin method of becoming a kayak.) For touring kayaks, I recommend a tough composite model simply because they can withstand running up on sandbars or scratching over oyster bars or being accidentally dropped at the boat launch. I look for durability in a boat and don't want something that needs babying.

For touring boats, consider storage capacity. Gear is usually stored in waterproof compartments with hatches. Look for watertight patches that close safely and securely. The larger the boat, the more room you will have. This is a matter of personal preference. Today, not only are there single kayaks, but also double kayaks, and even triple kayaks. Kayak anglers should shy away from these. Two people fishing from the same kayak is not a good idea. There's not enough boat with too much rod flying around. However, one person can guide, while the other person fishes, creating a superlative arrangement for the kayak angler.

Many touring kayaks come with a foot pedal-based steering system using a rudder. This allows for hands-free steering, which will avail a few

Kayaks make for good fishing vessels as seen here at Land Between the Lakes National Recreation Area.

more casts. Overall, kayak anglers need to be fussier when choosing their boats than do canoeists, since kayaks are more situation-specific. Surf the Internet and read reviews thoroughly to get an idea of what you want, and then go to a store that sells kayaks and try them out. Look for demo days at outdoors stores. Borrow a friend's kayak. A well-informed, careful choice will result in many positive backcountry kayak fishing experiences.

What about a whitewater kayak for fishing? This is a rare practice but it does allow you to go places neither a canoeist nor hiker can go. Pack ultralight, use a multipiece rod and small-lure kit, and be prepared to get out of the boat to actually fish.

Other Means of Backcountry Boat Fishing: Float Tubes and Rafts

Float tubes have been around since the 1940s and are used on lakes and slower streams. Once a mere circular tube with a built-in seat, most tubes today are U-shaped, with the angler facing into the open end of the U. Still others have two parallel inflatable pontoons. Floaters can accessorize with fins, rod holders, and more. Use a personal flotation

Fishing from a raft at New River Gorge, West Virginia

device (PFD) while float-fishing from a tube, which has the potential to get a hole popped in it.

Relatively few anglers fish from a whitewater raft but I have, on the New River in West Virginia, during fall. One of us steered the oar-frame model raft from the center, while two rode the river in bass-boat-like seats at each end, angling for smallmouth bass between the lively rapids. The raft was slow between rapids, but offered a good platform for fishing. The fall leaves were prime, and the smallies cooperated. Our large raft allowed us to bring camping gear. Overall, it was a great backcountry fishing adventure.

Canoe versus Kayak: Which One Should I Use When Backcountry Fishing?

Load It Up

Canoes are the most voluminous options while backcountry fishing, allowing you to carry lots of gear, including more than one fishing pole and a large tackle box. I have gone on backcountry fishing trips for up to 18 straight days in a canoe. This simply couldn't be done in any other type of boat.

The Wonderful World of Ice

Bringing a full-sized cooler is one of the biggest advantages of a canoe. Kayaks don't have the storage space. Coolers have come a long way the past few years and are more efficient than ever. You will see Five Day and Seven Day models, which, depending on conditions, mostly live up to their name. I have taken coolers on fishing trips for six days in the middle of a blistering Ozarks summer and left with ice.

Getting the Most Out of Your Ice

If you want to keep your ice as long as possible, the following tips will help. Keep the cooler covered while in the canoe. Much of the time while backcountry boat fishing you will be subjected to sun. Use a life vest or anything else that prevents direct sun access. Keep your vest on if conditions prohibit this, but a vest on top of a cooler is actually easy to access. Speaking of access, when putting the cooler in, face it with the lid opening toward the nearest paddler, that way you can get cold drinks and lunch while in the boat and/or put fish in for storage. Keep the cooler in the shade at camp, and continue covering it with the life vests. While at camp keep it away from the fire. Open the cooler only when necessary, and drain it in the morning and evening. But the best thing you can do is line your cooler with dry ice, which can be bought by the pound at big-box stores and major grocery stores.

Dry ice is frozen carbon dioxide, some as cold as −109.3°F. The name comes from its propensity to change from solid to gas, known as sublimation, without ever becoming a liquid. For best dry-ice results, throw regular ice in your cooler, chilling the cooler. Next, line the bottom of your cooler with dry ice, and put regular ice on top of the dry ice. Finally, store your goodies on top and enjoy the wonderful world of ice. One other thing: If drinking cold beverages, put in the day's quota of beverages in the cooler about three hours before you plan to drink them, and store the rest hot rather than trying to keep them all cold the whole trip. This saves cooler space and ice. Note that you can use a smaller cooler for your kayak. Just strap it on the outside. You may not look cool on the water, but you'll be drinking the cool beverages in camp.

Multiple Poles

The hot afternoon moved molasses slow on Georgia's Etowah River. We had been throwing spinners at the shaded shoreline of the river since noon, catching enough bream, along with an occasional bass, to keep our minds from drifting beyond the valley through which we floated. Then, out of the corner of my eye, a smallmouth bass gulped a bug from the surface. In a mere moment, I set down the rod tipped with a spinner and picked up my other rod, already rigged with a topwater Heddon. I tossed the frog imitation with rotating blade near where the bass had hit. As soon as the lure landed, the smallie slammed the frog, bringing forth that adrenaline that only a topwater strike can bring. I set the hook and was soon hauling in a fine bronzeback. If I'd had only one rod rigged, the opportunity to catch the bass on topwater would've passed.

Having two rods ready to go, I can easily switch my offerings. Before you can say swivel, I tell you that a swivel to help rapidly change lures doesn't work for me. In the clear backcountry waters that we seek, the fish are simply too smart to go for a lure attached to a swivel. Oh, some fish will hit, but it will be less than if fishing minus the swivel. Swivels also affect the action of the lure. The two-rod technique is reserved for paddling anglers, and of those, almost all in a canoe. If the fish aren't biting, you can try two lures and two techniques without spending all your time digging in the tackle box and changing lures, or as I call it, the ol' switcho chango. And with two anglers in the boat, y'all can be trying four different lures at once to see what will work.

The bow paddler generally keeps both poles forward, running parallel with the direction of the canoe, whereas the stern paddler keeps the poles sitting across the gunwales of the boat. Fishing with two rods isn't always advantageous. First, you have twice the rod in your boat to be tangled, swept away by a low branch, knocked off with the paddle, and to generally get in your way, especially on a gear-laden canoe camping excursion. The hooks of the lures on each pole can become intertwined.

I advise that novice backcountry and younger anglers stick with a single rod. It keeps things simple. However, experienced rod-throwers will be well served with twice the selection when it comes time to toss. Kayakers can use multiple poles if they have rod holders mounted onto their boat.

Twist and Turn

A canoe allows for greater freedom of movement. For better casting, you can shift around not only your head and shoulders but also your whole body, whether you are casting to the right or the left of the boat. It is easier to access your tackle box or anything else from a canoe than a touring kayak, where you are confined in a cockpit. Sit-on-top kayaks avoid this problem.

Easy Entry and Exit

Just as it is easier to move around in a canoe, it is easier to move into and out of a canoe than a kayak. This comes in handy when you're occasionally fishing from the shoreline or below rapids or other situations.

An Open Boat Can Fill with Water

A canoe is literally open to water coming in, whether from an accidental tipping or rain. When getting in and out of a canoe, water will often gather at the bottom of the boat and that can be troublesome or irritating. More dangerous, however, is when the canoe begins filling with water while going down a rapid, which brings the gunwales closer to the water and allows still more water to accumulate in the boat until the boat becomes entirely filled with water, spilling the paddlers and their contents. Kayaks, especially those with cockpits covered with a spray skirt, can handle waves no canoeist would ever even consider. This can come in handy if the weather turns foul and you are fishing big water or open coastal water. Whitewater kayaks can handle mega rapids.

Slow Travel

A canoe is much slower than a kayak when it comes to covering ground. You won't be zipping around in an open canoe. Kayaks, especially touring kayaks, are built to slice through the water. Canoes are primarily paddled with single paddles, rather than the more efficient double-bladed paddles used in kayaks. Kayaks cover more ground more quickly. This can come in handy if you are fishing widely separated holes on lakes or other bodies of water or if you like to cover ground between fishing opportunities. Lower profile sea kayaks, or sit-on-top kayaks, have less wind resistance and thus will be easier to paddle going against the wind, or when a wind blows one direction while you are fishing in another direction, forcing you to constantly adjust your position rather than going for fish. Because it takes less effort to move a kayak forward, someone trolling for fish will exert less effort in a kayak than a canoe.

Too Much Stuff

Because you can load so much stuff into a canoe you often do. These big loads can be not only weighty but also cumbersome. Many times I have seen paddlers piling their canoes so high with gear the rear paddler can hardly see the front paddler. Be careful arranging your loads. Stuff can and will get in the way of fishing!

Backcountry Boat-angler Necessities and Accessories

Types of Paddles

Wood is still holding on strong as a material for paddlers, though plastics dominate the market, especially lower end paddles, such as those used by outfitters, and also ultralight high-end paddles. Some cheap varieties combine a plastic blade with an aluminum handle. Bent shaft paddles are popular as well, though I don't recommend them for the backcountry angler. They are efficient as far as trying to get from point A to point B, but while fishing you are often drifting and turning, making constant small adjustments, turning the boat around and doing all sorts of maneuvers other than straightforward paddling in a line. Bent shaft paddles are poor when it comes to precision steering moves. How about a square versus rounded blade? I prefer a rounded blade for precision strokes, whereas a power paddler, maybe the bow paddler, will desire a square blade. Paddles can vary in length as well, generally from 48 to 60 inches. I recommend a shorter paddle for the stern paddler, because that is the person who makes the small adjustments in boat direction while fishing. A shorter paddle is easier to maneuver when making all these small adjustments, not only in the water, but also when shifting the paddle from one side of the boat to the next.

Kayak paddles are double-bladed, that is they have a blade on both sides, resulting in more efficient stroking. Kayakers seem more willing to part with a lot of money to use an ultralight paddle. Almost all kayak paddles are two-piece, snapping in the middle. This makes them easier to haul around, but more importantly it allows paddlers to offset the blades for more efficient stroking. Four-piece blades are not unusual either. Kayak blades are generally 6 inches by 18 inches, with paddles averaging between seven and eight feet in length. Weightwise, expensive paddles can go as low as 24 ounces or less, while average paddles are 30 to 40 ounces. Like anything, you get what you pay for. A paddle leash is a wise investment to prevent losing blade while casting.

Whether in a canoe or a sea kayak an extra paddle is a smart idea. It's easy to stow an extra paddle in the canoe but a kayak can be more troublesome. A four-piece paddle is easier to stow.

Life Vest

I admit to never wearing my life vest, or PFD, unless I feel threatened by the waters in which I ply. But I always have a PFD with me. In the bad old days, I would use anything that would meet Coast Guard standards just to get by. But now I carry a high-quality life vest, not only for safety but also for comfort. The better kinds, especially those designed for sea kayaking, allow for freedom of arm movement that is absolutely essential for the backcountry angler. Speaking of sea kayaking, that's when I have most often had on my PFD while backcountry fishing. Consider spending the extra money on a good life vest, not only for safety, but also for the ability to fish while having your vest on. Try them on at the store and feign casting.

Chair Backs

These hook onto the canoe seat to provide support for your back. I recommend the plastic models that cover most of your back, especially giving lower lumbar support. The more elaborate metal and canvas chair backs get in the way of casting out to the sides of the boat, as well as paddling. However, having no chair back on multiday trips can lead to Canoer's Back.

Dry Bags

Waterproof dry bags are one of those inventions that give modern backcountry fishers a major advantage over those of yesteryear. These dry bags, primarily made of rubber or plastic, have various means of closing, including zippers; the result is a watertight seal, keeping your gear dry as you travel backcountry fishing waters, whether they be oceanic or riverine. Gone are the more recent days of storing your gear in plastic bags or pickle canisters. There is simply no need with today's choices of dry bags, which can range from tiny, clear, personal-sized dry bags for storing things such as sunscreen, keys, bug dope, and a small box of lures, to massive rubber black holes with built-in shoulder straps and waist belts designed not only to keep your stuff dry, but to be carried on portages. Dry bags can be found at outdoor specialty retailers such as REI or fishing stores such as Bass Pro Shop.

Dry bags come in all sizes and shapes and are designed to fit in the tiny corners of a kayak or an open canoe. They can be long and thin to hold a tent, or wide and able to fit most anything. Kayakers should consider deck bags, which are attached to the top of the kayak just in front of the paddler. Store your lures and day-use items in there.

When nonportage canoe-camping, I use more dry bags, dividing what I store in them according to their contents. For example, I have one clear, personal-sized dry bag immediately at hand, another dry bag for clothes and sleeping bag, another for camping gear such as tents and camp chairs, and still another for cooking equipment and noncooler food. When in portaging country, I consolidate. Fewer bags are more efficient and the fewer individual items you are portaging the fewer you will forget. I hope someone enjoyed the 200 bucks worth of new lures I left in a tackle box at a portage in Ontario. Ditto for my brother's extra rod on Minnesota's Kawishiwi River. Speaking of that, while on long trips consider dividing your lure stash in two places, especially keeping new lures in their own area. This way if disaster strikes from a lure-losing spill into rapids, which has happened to me, or accidentally leaving your tackle box at a portage you won't be out of luck. Concerning dry bags, do not skimp on quality. Cheaper bags are thinner and will puncture more easily. Wet clothing or food can be disastrous on a backcountry fishing trip. Spend the extra bucks to get the good stuff. One final note: tie your dry bags down to your boat when you are going in rough water. That way your dry bags will stay with the boat if you take a spill.

Plastic Boxes

Plastic storage boxes, found at any mega-retailer, come in a variety of sizes and shapes. They are cheap, easily sit in the bottom of the canoe, and can double as a table. Use them to store items such as bread that

Packing Your Boat

An important rule for packing a canoe is to distribute the weight evenly, front to back and side to side. Too much weight in the front will cause the boat to dig and possibly fill with water when going through a rapid. Too much weight in the back will cause the boat to drag through shallows and steer poorly. Uneven side-to-side weight distribution is a major cause of tumping, as the canoe will list at precisely the wrong time. Factor the weight of the paddlers as well when distributing your gear in the canoe.

Backcountry anglers must consider not only weight but also placement. For casting purposes, keep your gear as low in the boat as possible. It keeps you from making an unintentional catch. This also helps when considering wind. A lower profile means less wind resistance for your loaded boat. And also try to keep things that might snag on your lure out of hooking range, such as a shirt taken off during a hot day. Create space for your tackle box and rods for easy fishing. Before departing on a major trip, do a dry run packing of your boat. This way you will get an idea where to place your gear and, more important, not have too much gear at the launch.

Packing a kayak can be more challenging. For starters, you have less room and have to pack your gear in sizes that will fit into the hatches of the boat. Once stored in these hatches, gear is generally safe but difficult to access. Therefore, try to anticipate what you will need during the day's fishing and paddling to avoid getting into the hatches of your boat.

For example, have all of your fishing gear, food and extra clothing needed for that day stored in the cockpit or on top of the kayak inside dry bags.

you don't want smashed. However, they are not nearly as waterproof as a rubber dry bag. Consider using these if you are on flat-water and are not portaging.

Portage Yokes

These are padded shoulder straps that you can mount to the thwart of a canoe. These aftermarket items aid greatly not only in comfort while portaging, but also balance.

Backcountry River-paddling Considerations

Checking Water Levels

Water levels are not only crucial for fishing a river, but also paddling a river. Fishing high waters can mean muddy waters, which eliminate angling for a fly/lure thrower. I have been midway on a long river trip and had a thunderstorm come up, eliminating our fishing for a couple of days until the water cleared. Muddy water is a higher possibility in spring and summer. Higher waters can also be more dangerous waters. I still remember launching on the Emory River in East Tennessee when the waters were flowing just below the treetops. We stupidly launched anyway, dumping the canoe on several occasions, and couldn't even fish while trying to keep the boat upright and worrying about our lives. I didn't check the water level before we left. Nowadays checking river levels is a matter of getting on the Internet. I prefer lower water levels while backcountry fishing. For starters, lower river levels concentrate the fish.

Secondly, less water means slower water, which allows for more comprehensive fishing because the river won't be blowing downstream. Lower water also means more still water and still water is where the fish will be holding, generally speaking. If wade-fishing, stay off high rivers. Backcountry creeks are generally higher in the spring and, combined with the chill of the water, make accidents and hypothermia a real possibility. Understand also that extreme high or low water levels will be throwing fish off their normal feeding patterns. So try to fish your river of choice within its historic flow realm for the time period you intend to visit.

Finding River Levels

The Water Resources Division of the United States Geological Survey measures water flows on most rivers in the United States at frequent intervals. The United States Army Corps of Engineers and various power companies collect similar information. These flows are recorded in cubic feet per second (cfs) and are available to everyone.

The key variable is the height of the river at a fixed point. Gauge houses, situated on most rivers, consist of a well at the river's edge with a float attached to a recording clock. The gauge reads in hundredths of feet. Rating tables are constructed for each gauge to get a cfs reading for each level. Other gauges are measured in height, given in feet. This information can be useful for backcountry anglers planning a trip. This gauge information can be obtained quickly, often along with recent rainfall. Make use of this information and compare it using guidebooks or Web sites such as **www.americanwhitewater.org** to find minimum and maximum runnable flow rates. Some river runnable rates have not been established. However, if you float your favorite river time and again, you can record the flow rates and river levels each time you float-fish the river and establish your own flow rates and levels at which the fishing and floating is best. USGS—Real-time Water Levels for the United States can be found on the Web at **waterdata.usgs.gov/nwis/rt.** This in-depth Web site has hundreds of gauges for the entire country updated continually, and graphs showing recent flow trends, along with historic trends for any given day of the year. The Internet is the greatest thing for backcountry float-fishers since lures were invented.

Arranging Shuttles

River trips require a shuttle. Setting up these shuttles is a pain but the payoff is getting to fish continually new waters in an ever-changing outdoor panorama. The closer you are to home, the more likely you are to be self-shuttling. When making a shuttle for the first time, do as much map work on the front end as possible. Many shuttles in backcountry areas require trips over dirt or gravel roads bouncing you and your boat all around. A wrong turn can eat up precious fishing time. Look for shuttle directions in outdoor guidebooks or on the Internet. Try to find safer landings such as those at state parks. Always remember to go to the takeout point first, leaving a car there, with the put-in point car following. When arriving at a landing, look around and gauge it for safety, especially scouring the ground for broken car glass. Go with your gut instinct. I have never had my car broken into while at a boat launch, but I have had it broken into at a hiking trailhead. Leave no valuables in your car. Take your keys with you and store them securely while you are floating. Consider finding a nearby homeowner or business and paying them to park. A few bucks can be worth peace of mind.

Self-shuttling versus Outfitters

Outfitters can save you the hassle of not only finding the put-in and takeout points, but also allowing you to leave your car in a safe, secure setting. Outfitters will also know something about the river you plan to fish and can help tailor a trip to suit your angling and camping desires. Of course, you will pay for this service. I frequently use outfitters for their local knowledge and to avoid the car-safety issue; plus, I don't have to drive two cars all the way to my chosen river. This especially helps on river trips that are far away from home. Everyone can pile in one car, saving gas and money, too. Finding shuttles can be as simple as an Internet search. Once you have found a few operators for your desired river, call each of them, because often they will operate different stretches of the river or only offer shorter shuttles. Backcountry anglers will generally be going on longer trips, especially farther away from home, and you want to make sure that the outfitter will go on a shuttle the length you desire. Don't be afraid to ask about prices, distances, reservations and especially fishing—everything from lures to species—but be very discerning with the fishing information. I have been duped by an outfitter concerning smallmouth fishing on an unnamed northern Kentucky river. Also ask about camping and potential crowds, especially if backcountry fishing during the weekend. Outfitter competence can vary. While on another unnamed river the outfitter got her car stuck on the way to the put-in, delaying our trip by hours.

Traveling with Your Boat

Boats, whether canoes or kayaks, need to be carried atop your vehicle en route to the water. How you load your boat depends on whether it is a canoe or kayak, what type of vehicle it is, and whether you have an after-market roof rack. No matter how you carry your boat, tie it down securely, for the sake of your boat and fellow drivers who will be endangered if your boat comes loose. I have seen a canoe fly off the car in front of me and what a boat will do to a car after sliding off the side of said car while still tied on. After cinching your boat down, drive a short distance and then pull over and recheck your tie job. I recommend using the flat straps with buckles, which are sold at most outdoor retailers and many big-box stores.

A top-quality aftermarket roof rack installed atop your vehicle makes for a much safer way to transport boats. Invest in one of these if paddling frequently. Roof racks can be customized to different types and numbers of boats as well. And don't skimp on tie-down straps either; these are what hold the boat to the rack.

The Fish

When it comes to fishing, it pays to know what you're looking for. The next section covers the most popular varieties of game fish that backcountry anglers seek.

Freshwater Fish

Cold-water Fish

Brook Trout. The brook is not a true trout, but a char. Endemic to the Appalachian Mountains of the East from North Georgia into Labrador and west into the Great Lakes states, this beautiful fish has been introduced throughout the West. Adults are greenish with the telltale wormlike markings on its back. The belly is usually white. Brookies can grow quite big in the far north, though your average backcountry angler will rarely see a brook trout bigger than a pound. Brooks prefer cold clear waters. Fly anglers will use nymphs and terrestrials, whereas small spinners work, too. When wade-fishing, proceed upstream with extreme stealth for these fighters.

Rainbow Trout. Rainbow trout are the most widely introduced cold-water fish in North America and are found just about anywhere any other trout exists. Native to the western slopes of the Rockies from California to Alaska, rainbows are spunky fighters and beautiful fish. As the name implies, a colorful band of pink, blue, and red extends along its sides,

Brook Trout

Rainbow Trout

overlaying a silvery sheen. The ocean running version of this fish is known as the steelhead. Rainbows fight hard and are known to jump. Rainbows are fairly aggressive feeders and take a variety of lures and flies. Rainbows prefer clear, clean water with a current, even though they are found in lakes. They eat small fish, worms, insects, and crustaceans, especially crawfish. Crawfish imitations can be deadly on rainbows. In streams, they will often be found in and around the fast moving water at the head of a pool.

Brown Trout. Brown trout, European natives, have been widely introduced to North American waters. Black, brown, and red spots are sprinkled over the brown base color of the fish. Browns can stand warmer and more turbid water than other trout, and are in every state and province in which trout can survive. They are also found in quieter, more still water, often in deep pools. They are not as easily fooled with flies as other trout, which are wary by nature. They are similar to rainbow trout in size, sometimes running a little larger but have similar fighting ability.

Brown Trout

Cutthroat Trout

Cutthroat Trout. This Western fish gets its name from the red lines on either side of its lower jaw. They are known to hybridize with other trout and are consequently harder to identify other than that one major characteristic, and they can come in with a variety of colors. They can be fooled with flies more easily than a brown. Spinners work well, too. My personal experiences with them forces me to put them below other trout in game quality, that is, how much it will fight. It seems to give up more readily than other salmonoids.

Golden Trout. This beautiful gold fish is the star of California's Sierra Mountains. It has been introduced into other California streams as well. A red stripe runs along the length of the fish, overlaying the gold base. These trout are generally small, especially in the fast-moving streams, though they will get bigger in slower streams and lakes. Goldens are fierce fighters for their size. I have fished Yosemite National Park among other places and fully enjoyed the golden trout experience. I recommend ultralight equipment with the smallest of flies and spinners. Look for pockets of slower water amid the crashing Sierra streams, though the fast water can make presentation more difficult.

Golden Trout

Fast-moving streams of California's Sierra Mountains harbor golden trout.

Dolly Varden and Bull Trout. Found in the northwestern United States and western Canada, these two cold-water fish are so similar they can be classified as one fish. They are usually silvery and/or olive green but take on the color of the habitat. Primarily found in Pacific Coast watersheds, they are both good fighters and can grow big. Bull trout are threatened by the introduction of nonnative species and are now in disjunctive populations; however, populations remain in portions of Oregon, Washington, Idaho, Montana, and Nevada. Bull trout are classified as a threatened species under the Endangered Species Act. Possessing a bull trout is strictly prohibited. Dolly Varden and bull trout are often confused with brook trout. The state of Washington has a catch phrase for this: "No black—put it back," alluding to the darker markings on the dorsal fin of the brook that are not present in a bull trout.

Lake Trout. Lake trout are found from Alaska throughout the Canadian provinces into Minnesota and across the Great Lakes region through New York and farther east through northern New England. "Lakers," as they are affectionately known, generally run five pounds or more and in Canada can get quite monstrous. They are strong fighters but because they are often found in deeper waters, the fights do not take acrobatic

Bull Trout

turns. In spring, lakers are often found in shallower waters. When the water warms, lakers go deep and can be caught only by deep trolling and casting. In the far north, however, they will stay in shallower water. In Canoe Country, I have used spoons with success for lakers and also have trolled in the bigger lakes for them.

Trout Habitats
Moving Water Habitats   Look for trout at the convergence of two water situations, whether it be changes in the water current or the underwater topography. For example, look where fast-moving water dumps from a rapid into a slower-moving pool. ❯

Lake Trout

Some streams offer multiple species of trout, such as brook, cutthroat, and brown.

Or cast where the underwater structure changes, such as behind a submerged tree or in a steep drop-off. This current change will most often be from faster to slower or in a seam where two currents merge, or where a small tributary flows into a larger stream.

Trout are like people. They prefer to sit still in a comfortable, safe place and wait for their food to come to them. When trout are not actively feeding, they will look for still water so they don't have to fight a current yet are able to spy food coming near them. For example, they may be hiding on the downstream side of a boulder or log structure or under overhanging banks. This way they can rest, yet still have a possibility of food flowing their way.

Trout Lake Habitats   Trout in currentless settings, such as lakes and ponds, must seek out their food, primarily along the shore line, where they swim in search of dinner. They will also go along "scum lines" where vegetational detritus gathers in windborne lines along a lake. Lake trout will often go deep in summer.

Northern Pike. Pike are the freshwater sharks of the North. These voracious, toothy fish are not only aggressive feeders, but they can get really big, too. Northern pike have a long body and a sloped head that opens to a long, big mouth. They are distributed throughout the far north of the entire globe. In the United States, pike range along the border states and into Canada, down to the Ohio Valley, the Great Lakes basin, and even into Missouri and Nebraska. Pike will savagely strike spoons, spinners, and topwater plugs. Pike respond to spoons that best replicate the size of the baitfish on which they are feeding.

They will lurk in sluggish streams and weedy lake shallows. As the water warms they will go slightly deeper. Pike generally hide in wait for

Northern Pike

prey, and then attack their target (or your lure) with a burst of speed. I even had one jump out of the water and hit a lure that was dangling off the edge of the canoe. Another time I hooked a pike that already had a snake hanging out of its mouth. Pike are slimy, so have a rag or fish glove at the ready when you bring one in.

Walleye. Primarily thought of as a northern species, walleye do extend into the far north of Canada, yet they reach down to the central and southern United States as far as Alabama. They are named for their strangely pearlescent eyes, which help them see and feed at night or in murky water, and they're also known for their long front teeth. They are highly prized eating fish but aren't known for fighting. They are found around underwater reefs and points on larger lakes and large, fairly slow

Walleye

67

rivers, primarily feeding at dusk and dawn. Backcountry anglers can often be seen jigging for walleye, though casting with jigs spinners and crank baits will also work. These fish rarely go for flies.

Other Cold-water Species. Arctic char are the northernmost of all game fish and stretch from the Pacific to the Atlantic across northernmost North America. These char will strike hard and mightily pull with their stout bodies. I have had a blast in Alaska fishing for them. Numerous species of salmon are throughout the cold waters of North America. Most of them are anadromous, cycling from freshwater to the sea back to the freshwater where they began. Once they leave the sea to spawn, they fight their way up stream becoming weaker and weaker, losing muscle tone and strength, eventually becoming food for omnivores such as bears. Whitefish is another category of salmonoid. These fish, including the mountain whitefish and cisco, primarily occupy the far north and border states of the United States. Of these, the most interesting is the Arctic grayling, known to ply the waters of the upper Missouri River drainage in Montana, including streams in Glacier National Park. They are good fighters. Their sail-like dorsal fin is their defining characteristic, and after catching one you will be shocked at the size of the fin relative to the size of the fish.

Warm-water Fish

Largemouth Bass. "Ol' bucketmouth" is native to eastern North America from southern Canada to northern Mexico, and the central United States east to the Atlantic coast, but has been introduced throughout America. Largemouth bass look very similar to their close cousin, the smallmouth; they are frequently found in the same waters. To tell the two apart, look at the closed mouth: if it extends back beyond the back of the eye, the fish is a largemouth; if it goes only to the middle of the eye, it's a smallmouth. Color is also an indicator. Largemouth tend to be greener, whereas smallies can have a bronze hue. Though found in rivers, largemouths reach their greatest size in lakes of the Southeast and more recently California. These aggressive fish like warm, shallow water and plenty of vegetation. When fishing for largemouth, work as close to cover as possible. Plastic worms are the time-honored lure, though spinners and topwater plugs work, too, as well as crank baits and jigs. Fly-fishers use streamers and popping bugs.

Smallmouth Bass. A favorite species of the backcountry angler, these are brown or bronze on the sides with three to five dark lines radiating back

Largemouth Bass

from the eye. Smallies love clear, rocky, fast-flowing streams and rivers and need cooler waters than their largemouth cousins do. Anglers should seek waters with gravel riffles, deep pools, and cover such as large rocks or submerged trees. In lakes, smallmouth are shallow in spring and then move to deeper water as the water warms. They then hold around structure and shade. Look around points and along drop-offs and ledges. They will also hold around vegetation, where forage and cover is available. Ultralight spin casting with floating crawfish, topwater lures, and spinners can produce loads of fun whether you're on a lake or river.

Smallmouth Bass

Rock Bass

Rock Bass. The rock bass isn't really a bass but, rather, part of the sunfish family. Rock bass, also known as redeye or goggle eye, favor clear, cool to warm waters over a gravel or rocky bottom with some vegetation, and also shorelines with rocks of varied depths. The distinctive red eye and a stout body are its defining characteristics. Rock bass, an underrated species, have spread their range through both introduction and self-expansion. It can be argued that—pound for pound—these fish, which generally run under a pound, are the hardest fighters backcountry anglers will encounter. Redeyes will take all manner of spinners but love crawfish imitation plugs. Fly-fishers will have success with popping bugs and large wet flies.

Panfish. Panfish is an all-inclusive term covering sunfish such as bream, bluegill, shellcracker, and pumpkinseeds, among other subspecies. Often they're the first fish young anglers catch with a worm suspended below a bobber attached to a cane pole. Backcountry fishers will find them primarily in warm-water creeks and rivers. Trough introduction they are found throughout the United States and much of Canada, being highly adaptive to varying temperatures and water conditions. Most slabsiders are under a pound and use their broad build to fight the good fight. In summer, they will strike throughout the day, keeping the action going. Fly-fishers will use popping plugs and have a ball. Spin-fishers will have most success with spinners but don't be surprised when slabsiders hit plugs half their size. Panfish can

Panfish

school together and are often found close to the shoreline structure such as tree roots, rocks, and vegetation.

Saltwater Fish

Ladyfish. Nicknamed the poor man's tarpon, ladyfish are fun to catch whether you're using a fly rod or conventional tackle. Slender and silver with big eyes, ladyfish are bony to the extreme. When hooked, they will jump multiple times. Be careful when you get them close to the boat, because they will tear off on another run or flip crazily just as you are trying to grab them. They will take all manner of lures, including topwater plugs, gold spoons, and jigs. Fish average one to two pounds in size and if you get a bigger one you'll be in for a great fight. They seem to be all over saltwater backcountry and can turn bad days into good ones. Wear a

Ladyfish

Mangrove Snapper

fish glove on when you land one, because they're slimy and can hook you while still flailing around.

Mangrove Snapper. Mangrove snapper are most often caught using bait but will also go for artificials. Inshore, where backcountry anglers will be, snappers will be found near mangrove roots, along tidal creeks and bigger tidal rivers. They are colored dark brown or gray with reddish or orange spots in rows along their sides. Two canine teeth protrude from the upper jaw. Scientifically known as a gray snapper, it is found throughout the Gulf of Mexico and up the Atlantic coast to Massachusetts.

Redfish. More accurately known as red drum, this hard-fighting game fish with the black tail spot can be caught on flies and with spinning gear.

Redfish

Jigs, plugs, and gold spoons are the favored lures when going for reds, whereas fly rodders will use large streamers. This tasty fish is highly sought and has strict limits protecting them. Redfish can be found around oyster beds, mangrove roots, and in shallow waters above mud or grass bottoms. Geographically, reds range along the East Coast from Massachusetts south to Florida and throughout the Gulf of Mexico.

Sea Trout. Sea trout are a favorite backcountry game fish of mine. They have a wide range and distribution, are fairly easy to catch but can put up a fight; plus, they taste great! When you catch one you will often catch another, since they swim in schools. Sea trout are found throughout the Gulf of Mexico and up the Atlantic Coast to Cape Cod, Massachusetts. They are most often found in shallow grassy flats, but can be found up tidal rivers, in bays, and off points where there is moving water. Sea trout can be caught while trolling, using shallow running plugs. They will also bite jigs, spoons, and will even go for topwater presentations.

Tarpon. Backcountry anglers are usually not prepared for a tarpon strike. I have never landed a big tarpon from a canoe or kayak. Usually the tarpon struck when I was fishing for something else, and I enjoyed a few leaps and bounds before it cut the line. The real question is what would I do if I got a "silver king," which can go more than 300 pounds, to my boat? Smaller tarpon can be lip-locked, that is, grasped on the lower lip between your thumb and forefinger. Quickly release the tarpon, as it is inedible and very vulnerable when out of the water. Primarily found in the warmer waters of the western Atlantic, tarpon can range up to

Sea Trout

Tarpon

Canada and down the South American coast. They venture into freshwater rivers, too.

Snook. Often likened to the saltwater version of a largemouth bass, snook are found in the Everglades and around Padre Island National Seashore. They're silvery with a darker coloration on their upper side, but their defining feature is the thin black stripe that runs from the head to the tail. Snook like to hide and ambush their prey. This coastal fish can also be found anywhere there is moving water, such as the mouths of creeks, tidal river banks, and along beaches. Once hooked, snook can

Bob Care - Florida Keys NMS   *Snook*

Jack Crevalle

make powerful runs into underwater structure such as fallen trees. They also jump. Snook can be lip-locked, unlike most other ocean-going fish.

Jack Crevalle. This aggressive fish uses its flat silvery-white-and-yellow body for strong runs, and strikes all manner of lures from gold spoons to many types of flies. Jacks are found in tidal rivers, river mouths, bays, and points where the tide is moving the water. They range from Nova Scotia down the Atlantic Coast into the Gulf of Mexico and beyond to South America. When handling a jack, grab it where the tail and body meet.

Surf-fishing

Backcountry anglers, especially when traveling by boat or backpacking places such as North Carolina's Cape Lookout National Seashore, can surf-fish. They will be looking for places of water runoff, eddies where currents meet, or where birds are diving into schools of baitfish. Hopefully, a school of saltwater fish will begin to chase the baitfish. The challenge of surf-fishing is that it requires its own tackle. You can't just simply start using your average saltwater spinning reel and rod and expect to catch fish; however, don't let that stop you from casting plugs from any backcountry beach.

Surf rods are stout and long, from 10 to 12 feet. These hefty rods are needed in order to throw the heavy weights, bait, and the heavy lines on the far side of the breaking surf, making long casts. Match your reel with these rods. To rig a rod, a heavy sinker is placed on the end of the line, then the hook and leader are attached to the primary line above the heavy sinker. These sinkers are usually pyramid in shape. Bait can be a problem for backcountry surf anglers. Squid, bloodworms, live fish, sand fleas, and more are used. However, you can use lures especially after you run into a feeding school of fish. Try topwater plugs and spoons. Use a sand spike when surf-fishing. This keeps your rod upright and will give resistance when you aren't holding the rod yourself.

Fishing Techniques

When discussing fishing techniques, first determine by what means you will be fishing, whether on foot or by boat. If fishing by boat, you will be fishing still water or be going *downstream* on a waterway. If fishing by foot you will likely be going *upstream* a river or creek, the opposite direction of boating anglers. Fish generally face upstream when searching for food. So whether you are coming up behind them while wading, or floating down toward them is an important distinction in how to cast for your quarry. That being said, the fish will be holding and feeding where they will be whether you are coming up from behind them or coming downstream toward them. In general, fish will hang around areas that meet two criteria:

1. Food, where food is plentiful and easiest to catch—minnows, crayfish, insects, and so on.
2. Cover, where they can hide and/or not be seen. Yep, food and shelter, just like us!

Where Fish (Usually) Are:
under or behind a log
hidden among underwater tree roots
the downstream side of a rock
in a deep hole
in the shade
in an eddy line where two currents converge
along the edge of a current
behind submerged rocks in the deepest part of a rapid
along the shore with cover of some type
in a deep pocket amid shallow waters
on the edge of weeds and grasses
in pockets of different-sized rocks
along a scum line
around points
along drop-offs and ledges

Where Fish (Usually) Aren't:
in the middle of a river
in wide shallows
in the strongest flow of a rapid
beneath a sheer rock bluff
in front of an object facing the flow of the water
in open featureless water
in still water overflows not connected to the main body of water
in the open sun
along featureless mud banks
anywhere after a cold front

Flies or Lures

Choice of flies or lures is your opportunity to make or break your fishing trip. The wrong fly or lure in the wrong place can mean no fish, while the right one in the right place can mean a backcountry fishing trip to remember. When choosing flies and lures you need to know not only which kind but also how many to get. For example, if you are going out on a five-day river float and you will be throwing many topwater plugs, count on losing a few. Or if you are using flies on a bigger western river while backpack-fishing, you may not be able to retrieve them all. And then there are the lures that get away when fish break the line. If you are fishing hard, factor in losing a fly or lure a day, at least. Keep extras of your favorites.

Fly-fishing

Flies

A fly—a small artificial lure made from hair, feathers, thread, and other materials—is designed to imitate an insect or other bait for which fish would naturally pursue. Once used primarily for cold-water fishing such as trout, fly-fishing has expanded to warm and salt water. Most flies have just one hook. They come in a dizzying array of patterns. Some anglers will tie their own flies. It is a great activity during the colder times when the fish aren't biting, and is considered part of the fly-fishing experience. Tying flies takes patience, but they are much cheaper than when purchased in the store. The fly you ultimately use depends on the type of fish you are trying to catch, when you are fishing, where you are fishing, and what type of fly-fishing you want to do. When you fly-fish, it's the line that provides the weight needed to cast your fly and also to make your retrieve

Popular flies (clockwise from bottom center): pop-n-bug (bass bug), muddler minnow (streamer), Chernobyl ant (terrestrial), Tellico nymph, wolf dry fly, wooly bugger, clauser minnow (streamer), copper John (nymph)

or presentation. In contrast with spin-fishing, your lure provides the mass and weight to allow you to cast to the fish, and therefore you have to use your reel to retrieve and present the lure.

Dry Flies

These flies are called "dry" because they float on the surface of the water and are designed to imitate a floating insect. A very light hook is used to help it float. To keep the fly floating you may have to treat it or dry the fly between uses. A popper, made from cork, floats also, and is used to catch panfish and bass.

Wet Flies

Wet flies are designed to imitate underwater bugs; therefore, they do not float on the water's surface. Also, bigger wet flies can be made to imitate critters such as crawdads. It can be argued that more than imitating a particular insect, a wet fly is designed to imitate the motion of an insect under water.

Streamer

Streamers are larger flies and may be considered a subcategory of wet flies. Streamers, which are long and narrow, are often tied to imitate a minnow or injured baitfish. And as with other lures, the larger flies are designed to catch the larger fish. Streamers sometimes have more than one hook and are often used to catch warm-water species such as bass. Retrieves with streamers are sometimes erratic, in order to imitate the actions of an injured fish.

Nymph

Consider a nymph to be another type of wet fly. A nymph is an insect that is changing from its larval stage, coming out of its cocoon, and is particularly desirable, as it rises to the surface before hatching. Some nymphs will be weighted to keep them under water. Bobbers—strike indicators—as they are known in the fly-fishing world to distinguish them from the fishing-with-bait-from-the-bank-set, are used to help the angler know the fish is biting the nymph, as the current is giving a tug as well.

Terrestrial

A terrestrial is what its name indicates—a bug born on the land that has accidentally gotten into the water, such as an ant, beetle, or grasshopper. Terrestrials may be tied as dry or wet flies, and when cast will be made to land a little harder on the water—as a grasshopper would if it mistakenly ended up in a stream instead of on the land.

Fishing and Weather

The skies darkened overhead as we traveled downriver. We continued to fish as the path of the potential thunderstorms could as easily go out of our way as they would go directly over our heads. The warm air cooled and we decided to get off the river, having caught more than our share of trout. We were one day into a multiday trip and were looking forward to much success in the coming days. The next morning was surprisingly cool, which unbeknownst to us was going to affect the fishing from here on out. A front had blown through and the fish simply turned off. We struggled to get our limit the next day, as we were relying on fish for dinner. Weather is a huge consideration for anglers. Fish are notoriously subject to cold fronts blowing through, among other weather considerations. During the hot days of summer, fish will often bite only in the morning and evening. Fish will bite immediately after thunderstorms, which have pushed a lot of food into streams with their sudden flows. Rain makes using topwater baits difficult. On cooler days, fish will sometimes be found out of the wind sunning in shallows. Before embarking on a trip, consider the forthcoming weather predictions and how they will relate to your fishing.

A good base kit for spin-fishers (clockwise from top left): Mepps Agila, Floating Rapala, Rebel Crawfish, Panther Martin, Heddon Baby Torpedo

Spin-fishing

To sum it up, spin-fishers will be using a shorter rod and a bigger lure than a fly-fisher will. As previously mentioned, the lure provides mass and weight to allow for casting, presentation, and retrieval, whereas in fly-fishing the line provides the weight for casting and presentation. As far as which spin-fishing lures to take, stream regulations will dictate alteration of the following suggestions, but this is a base list of lures from which to work. The first choice is a ⅛-ounce gold Panther Martin spinner with orange trim. Gold seems to work everywhere a lure will work. You can see a gold spinner run through the water and consequently see the strike. That's half the fun. I would have at least three of these at all times, even on a day trip. Panther Martin spinners are superior because of design. The blade is mounted directly on the spinner shaft, forcing a spin no matter the speed of the current or your retrieve, whereas the blades of other spinner are hooked to metal that is hooked to the shaft. Consider making one of your Panther Martins a ¼-ounce lure. This way you can cast farther, and bigger lures catch bigger fish (but not always more fish). The smaller lure, ¹⁄₁₆ ounce, can be prohibitively small, especially when it comes to distance casting. They are preferred only on the smallest of trout streams. Secondly, I would have a gold Mepps Agila, dressed with a brown

Kent Roller's catch on West Virginia's Greenbrier River, using a Rebel Crawfish

"squirrel tail," which disguises the hook and gives added action. It is tried and true, outlasting trendy lures. I always take three plugs. The first is a floater/diver Rebel Crawfish. I recommend the Teeny Wee Crawfish and the Wee Crawfish for most backcountry destinations.

Speaking of two different sizes, what about two different fish, two different sizes, on one crawfish? My pal Kent Roller and I were on West Virginia's Greenbrier River when he threw a crawdad into a midstream hole. He got a strike right away, and to his surprise pulled up a small-mouth bass and a rock bass, each latched onto their own treble hook on the crawdad! I have had my own "double-doubles" as well.

When it comes to trout I have better luck with the smaller size craw-fish. Also, as with all lures I'm a fan of realistic colors. Go with red/brown or green/brown. This can be used for trout, panfish, and bass. It can be operated as a topwater lure and for deeper action. If you aren't having luck, try reeling at different speeds, and bang off rocks to re-create the erratic movements of a crawfish. Sometimes, an ultraslow retrieve will bring in the fish when nothing else is working. The second plug would be a gold Floating Rapala, 3⅛ inches, with two treble hooks. This can be effectively used as topwater bait in lakes and in still water on streams, and can also bring out some big fish from larger stream pools. It can also draw in trout and smaller bass in moving water. The third and final plug in the arsenal would be a Heddon Baby Torpedo with the blade on back. Specifically, I use the green and white baby bass and the green and yellow bullfrog. These can be deadly when operated correctly in still water, but is much less effective in moving water. Sometimes, while stream-fishing, if I get to a particularly large hole, I will change to a plug from a spinner to see if I can catch the big one. The best multiuse plug from the above is the crawfish. The above arsenal has evolved over the years. I was once a big fan of Roostertail spinners but found the blades less effective in waters of varying current speeds. If you want more variety in your spinners, vary your colors, including silver-based Panther Martins and Mepps. For faster moving waters, you may also want to include a Panther Martin with a wider, heavier body.

Fishing Techniques by Boat

While floating downstream on a river you should be constantly scanning the forthcoming water for holding spots, where a fish will be waiting in search of a tasty morsel coming its way. Don't worry so much about spooking the fish by boat as you would by foot; canoes and kayaks glide over the water and are much less obtrusive than a motorboat.

When casting toward the shore, try to get your fly/lure as close as possible to the nexus of land and water. At the shore, fish will think that your offering may be a bug or something that has come from the land, such as a grasshopper, as well as potentially being something that lives in the water, such as a minnow. Try to get a little bit of an arc while casting so the lure will plop down on the water, alerting the fish of potential food. However, don't arc it so high that its landing will scare away the fish. Sometimes, low branches prevent the ideal presentation. Other times you may throw a little too far and hit land—go ahead and pop your lure back into the water and continue your retrieve.

Before casting, look for underwater obstructions such as rocks or fallen trees. You will want to throw your lure to avoid these obstructions, but you want to cast your lure near the obstructions to take advantage of their fish-holding potential. When casting as the boat is floating downstream, you must calculate the speed at which to retrieve the lure with the speed of the boat floating downstream, while simultaneously factoring in these water structures. Do not cast somewhere that will

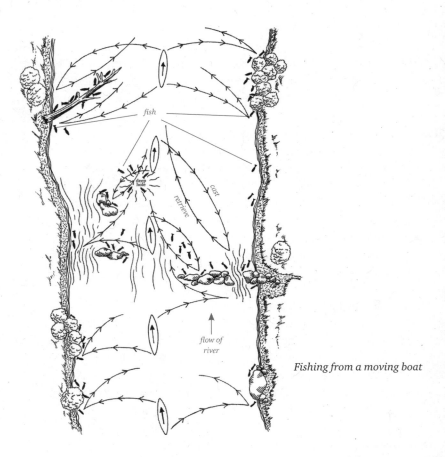

Fishing from a moving boat

force a retrieve through fallen brush or over exposed rocks. You will likely get hung, and if you catch a fish you won't be able to get it back to the boat. An ideal cast would plop the lure within one foot of the shoreline, in front of where you think a fish might be, not on top of its head. A fish will strike something presented in front of it before it will strike something atop it. If a fish doesn't strike immediately, begin retrieving your lure on either side of the obstruction, whether it be a rock or log. Each side of the obstruction, whether upstream or downstream, has its own advantages. When a lure that is being retrieved on the upstream side of an obstruction makes the curve to get around the end of the obstruction, this is where a fish from behind the obstruction will strike, making an ambush. If you are retrieving your offering on the downstream side of the obstruction, the fish will be more likely to see your lure and can also strike then. Be careful when casting your lure onto the far side of a log—if

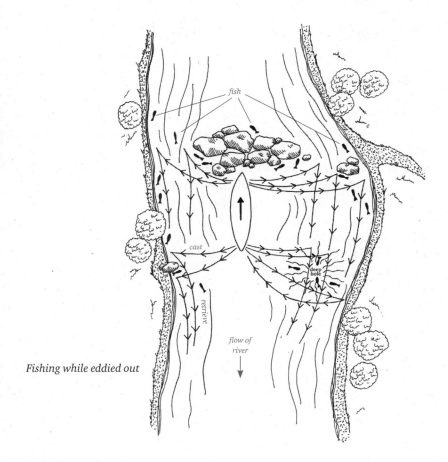

fish

cast

retrieve

deep hole

flow of river

Fishing while eddied out

the fish strikes you will have a hard time pulling it over the log with the ultralight tackle normally used by backcountry anglers.

Other times you will want to stop the boat entirely to fish. This is often done at a rapid. Once safely through the rapid turn the boat and eddy out as soon as you can find some still water. Then cast into the rapid or other still water areas adjacent to the moving water. If you are catching fish and having a lot of action be patient and work the area thoroughly. It may be the highlight of your day.

A cast doesn't have to be long to be a good cast. Whether you are in an eddy or moving, look for fish-holding areas close to the boat and don't be dissuaded from tossing as close as five feet away for a fish. Remember that placement of your boat to get yourself in the right position is as important as placing your lure in the right spot. The stern paddler should always be thinking about keeping the boat the proper distance from the shoreline and also looking downstream for potential hazards as well as potential fishing spots.

Techniques on Foot

Fishing on foot is an entirely different story. You always want to fish upstream on moving water. This way you are coming up from behind the fish, therefore all fishing techniques assume wading upstream. The general wade-fishing technique can be broken down into three steps: approach, position, and presentation. When wade-fishing, you are stalking fish, just as the fish you are stalking are stalking their prey. Wear clothes that blend with the environment. Try to be as quiet as possible when working upriver. Always look ahead to see where you think the fish might be, and then work your way upstream in order to not give away your presence. When in the water, move slowly, making the least amount of turbulence. Try to stay on the edge of pools, so your reverberations will not reach the fish. Do not stare into where you think the fish might be. I fully believe that creatures can sense one another's presence. And your presence can be given away by focusing too hard on where the fish is. Instead, size up the pool and appreciate the surrounding scenery until you are ready to make your cast. Here are some other approach thoughts: stay low—the higher you are, the more likely a fish can look up to see you; avoid disturbing overhanging tree limbs and brush—the movement of this vegetation will put fish on alert; stay behind the fish—if you walk to the head of a pool and fish downstream then fish will be alerted to your presence.

Once you have made your way to a good fishing hole, look for the best spot to drop your lure, and find the best position to make the presentation. Does your chosen position have good footing? This is important because when you hook a fish you don't want to slip and fall. Are there obstructions in the way such as limbs overhead or beside the stream? Can you make multiple casts into multiple potential holding spots in the hole from the position? Can you land a fish from your spot? Can you get your chosen spot without alerting the fish? All else being equal you want a relatively shallow spot adjacent to a gravel bar or dry land of some sort, a place without any nearby vegetation obstructions and a place where you can maneuver around in case you hook a big one. Do not fish from atop a high rock—you can't get a good cast in the water and the fish will see you as well.

A good approach to a good position should be followed by good presentation. Look over the fishing hole and make your first cast your best one to the best spot—the money cast. The biggest fish will be occupying the

flow of
river

deep
hole

deep
hole

Where fish will be holding

best spots in the pool per the pecking order of fish size. After your best first cast you can then try to cover all the other potential areas. By the way, if you think a fish is in a certain spot and it didn't hit on the first cast, try again, but most strikes will occur on the first cast.

When casting, remember that fish will be holding on the edges of moving water or in deeper holes looking toward the moving water for a tasty morsel to float by. Therefore you will want to cast your lure into the moving water and run it by the places where fish may be holding, such as the downstream side of a rock, amid a fallen tree, or the base of a deep pool. For warm-water species you can cast directly into the still waters with more success.

Before making your presentation, position yourself on one side of the stream and throw your fly/lure upstream and across to the far bank. As you retrieve, you will be pulling your lure downstream and back toward you. While reeling let your lure get downstream of you. Fish will often

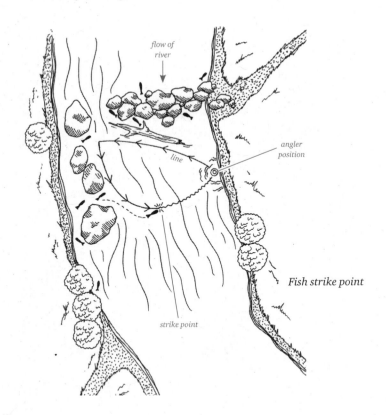

flow of river

line

angler position

Fish strike point

strike point

bite at the exact point at which you begin to retrieve the lure back upstream. Why? The fish is bigger than the bait and knows it can outswim its prey. When the prey turns upstream it will be fighting the current and the bigger fish knows it has a swimming strength advantage and thus will strike at that point. (Imagine an adult chasing a child on level ground and chasing the child uphill. If the adult didn't catch the kid on level ground it will catch the kid on the uphill.) So at the point the lure begins to turn upstream be prepared for a strike. This is especially true on fast moving Western streams. This same principle works in the ocean for game fish going against the tide after bait. *Note:* In moving water everything happens fast. Be prepared to set the hook when the fish bites.

In general, while retrieving a lure I will reel slightly faster than the flow of the current. However, you may vary the speed your reel within one cast, reeling slow in a slower section and speeding up your reel as your lure crosses a faster section. If the fish aren't biting, vary your retrieve, alternating fast and slow to make the lure rises toward the surface and dips down back toward the bottom, in jig fashion. You may want to work some lures slowly, or in a herky-jerky fashion, to replicate a wounded critter, which means easy pickings for game fish. And if you see a fish following your lure, speed up. This is the natural reaction of prey to a predator. If you slow down, waiting for the fish to bite, it will sense something is wrong and give up the chase.

Fishing is a numbers game. The more casts you make the larger number of fish you will catch. You can definitely catch fish with the less than ideal catch. Be active to maximize results. Fishing is also a mind game. Believe you are going to catch fish, believe in your techniques, and expect to catch fish. Be confident. Those who expect to catch fish catch more fish than those who don't.

Handling Your Fish

As backcountry anglers we appreciate superlative scenery in our watery getaways. But that doesn't mean we don't want to catch fish. We do! And once we get one on the line and into our possession we want to be able to handle the fish with care. Here are some tips for handling and releasing fish: Avoid playing the fish to exhaustion. If you don't want to keep the fish, or the fish is smaller than legal minimum, release it immediately and gently back into the water. When unhooking the fish avoid handling it too much. The fish slime you get on your hands is a protective mucus covering that prevents infection. Do hold the fish firmly. Dropping a fish on the ground or the bottom of your boat decreases its survivability. Grab smaller fish around their midsection. Grab largemouth fish by the lower jaw with your thumb and forefinger, a lip lock. Avoid putting your fingers into the gills or eye sockets of fish. Large and toothy fish should be grasped using a fish glove. This way you can get a solid grip on the fish before dislodging hooks. Pliers are necessary for quick hook disgorging. Try to back the hook out if possible, rather than pulling it through the fish. Barbless hooks are easier for you to unhook the fish and are easier on the fish itself.

Keeping Fish

It was the first backpack-fishing trip of the year. We arrived at the campsite and hastily readied our poles and lures. We had just started an eight-night trip in Washington's Wenaha-Tucannon Wilderness. My friend Tom Rodgers dashed up trail to try his luck on Crooked Creek, while I rushed down the Wenaha River to waters to I had secretly scouted on the hike up. The fishing rodeo was on. "A glorious day to be trout-fishing," I thought to myself as I stepped into the chilly water, under a bold blue sky, and made my first cast.

"Why aren't the fish biting?" I thought to myself two hours later. I couldn't ask for better scenery though: the clear creek and tumbling cascades amidst pure wilderness—but I wanted a multihued rainbow trout. Just then Tom walked up with two shiny rainbows in hand. Dinner was coming, but not easily. Tom had scouted some potential fishing holes and let me in on his findings, rekindling my excitement. Together we ambled upstream in the warm sunshine, spending the balance of the afternoon fishing above camp. I pulled a handsome 'bow out of a slow pool flowing past a tall rock ledge below some rapids. The sun left the valley, hastening our return to camp. But our frying pan needed more fish. With determination I grabbed my pole and decided to try a flat riffle in front of camp. I cast my line and caught three trout in succession. What fortune! You would think the water near camp would be hard fished. Trout are superseded only by women as the world's most enigmatic creatures.

Catching and keeping fish when you need them doesn't always happen, but if you decide to keep them, have a strategy. When backcountry fishing by boat, use a stringer. On warm days allow more stringer length so fish can get under shade of boat, and have a stringer for each end of the boat. Putting fish in your cooler is another way to keep them until camp. If doing this, I prefer to gut the fish shortly after catching it. That way, the fish takes up less room in the cooler. However, I generally avoid using a cooler so as not to foul it up with fish smell. If you do, have a separate plastic bag or two and put your fish inside the bag, then inside the cooler and not directly on the ice. Ideally, it's nice to catch your fish late in the afternoon, that way you don't have to keep them as long, but we've all thrown fish back early, thinking we would catch them later, and ended up at the campsite with no fish. It can be especially troublesome carrying fish on a portage between lakes, because they are out of the water for a relatively long period and become stressed, if not dead.

If I'm walk-fishing up a stream and plan on backtracking to camp or the trailhead after fishing I will store my keepers in the stream and then get them. After catching one, I will cut a small live limb about 12 to 14 inches long, rhododendron for example, making sure that one end of it has two branches making a Y. Then I run the limb through the fish's lower lip. I find a nice slow part of the stream that is deep enough for the fish, stick the end without the Y into the streamside rocks or sand, and cover the end stuck in the stream bottom with more rocks. Then I'll lay a rock or two on the Y end of the stick. The Y prevents the fish from getting out from the streamside end of the stick. Then I walk up the bank to the adjoining trail and mark the spot with an X of rocks or sticks. This way I know where I left the fish. And using this method, I can fish upstream unencumbered by a stringer or creel, while keeping the fish alive.

However, if you first walk downstream and then fish your way back up to camp, you must carry your fish with you. But this method has its advantages. Because you are doing your walking on the front end, you simply end your angling day at camp, whereas the person fishing upstream fishes until they are tired, then has to walk back to camp, plucking their fish as they return.

Speaking of creels, I have one in my basement that I've never used. Creels have not only fallen out of favor with me but everyone else, or so it seems. You can find creels on the Internet, but most of them are sold as antiques.

Anglers Code of Ethics

Here's a little food for thought—the Anglers Code of Ethics as put forth by the state of Florida.

The ethical angler

1. Supports conservation efforts.
2. Practices effective catch-and-release of fish that are unwanted or prohibited to retain.
3. Doesn't pollute; recycles and disposes of trash.
4. Practices safe angling and boating, by following the laws and using common sense practices to prevent injury to themselves, others or property.
5. Learns and obeys fishing and boating rules and regulations, and purchases the appropriate licenses.
6. Respects other anglers' and boaters' rights.
7. Respects property owners' rights and does not trespass.
8. Shares fishing knowledge and skills.
9. Doesn't release live bait into waters or spread exotic plants and fish.
10. Promotes ethical sportfishing and encourages others to reconnect on the water.

Fishing Licenses

It was day three of a five-day trip. The fish were biting and were going to be part of our dinner that night. Because it was Saturday, more anglers were on the river. As we floated downriver other anglers were passing the word that a game warden was downstream checking licenses. We had nothing to worry about, because we were completely legal. Sure enough, the warden asked us to pull over, produce our licenses, and show our fish. We then went on our way.

When traveling far to execute a backcountry fishing adventure, the first adventure may be getting a fishing license. To ease things, I suggest using the Internet to get your fishing license through the department of natural resources for your chosen state. Then you can print out a receipt of your license, or the license itself, saving yourself the trouble of finding a store that is open that has a fishing license. Make sure you get all necessary stamps along with your license. Your monies go to enhancing the fishery resources of the state where you got your license.

Backcountry Campsites

Finding a Camp by Foot

I was in the midst of an 11-night solo backcountry fishing trip in Oregon's Eagle Cap Wilderness. It was the eighth day and I'd spent much time in the high country where the fish had been biting in the alpine lakes—but so had the mosquitoes. Most of the other backcountry anglers had been at those lakes as well. I decided to look for a little more solitude and hoped a change of elevation would also cut down on the bugs. I left Steamboat Lake and dropped down to the North Minam River. The lower end of the meadows was mine and I found a riverside tree copse to camp under. I cast a line for the many brook trout in the river, meeting with ample success. Upon returning to the lovely, bugless campsite in the evening, I concluded it is important to have a good camp as well as a good fishing destination when you're deep in the outback.

The author angles at an alpine lake deep in Oregon's Eagle Cap Wilderness.

Minimally speaking, a backcountry campsite requires two things: a flat spot and water. Because backcountry anglers will naturally be near water, the primary requirement is a flat spot. Beyond that, look for natural characteristics of the land to help you deal with the situations at hand. For example, you may want an open, breezy location if the insects are troublesome. You may want a sheltered location if the winds are howling. You may want shade if it's hot or ample fallen wood for a fire if it's cold. Let your surroundings help keep you more comfortable in camp.

From this point you begin to look for other characteristics that will make your campsite not only functionally desirable but also aesthetically pleasing. I often like to set up camp near a great fishing hole that I can access quickly from camp. Or why not go for a view if you can get it?

Some backcountry fishing destinations have designated campsites that require a backcountry permit, such as Yellowstone National Park, or have specific camping rules such as Shenandoah National Park. Other places, such as national forests wilderness areas, are more freewheeling. Still others have designated campsites where you can stay at without a permit, such as Wisconsin's St. Croix National River. Before you begin a trip, check into specific camping regulations.

National parks often require camping permits but also offer scenic angling such as this at Yellowstone National Park.

There are also some safety considerations. Look around for widow makers—dead standing trees that may fall during a storm. This actually happened to us on a fishing trip in Alaska but luckily the tree, while falling, was slowed down by hitting other trees before it plunged down onto our shelter. We considered ourselves very lucky. Don't get so close to a water source that your camp may flood. For that matter, stay off any river in flood conditions whether you are going overnight or not. When in bear country, take ample precautions and hang your food.

Setting Up Camp

Think of your campsite as a bedroom, kitchen, living room, and bathroom. Each area has its own distinctive characteristics that you will be seeking. When setting up your sleeping quarters, whether they are in the open, under a tarp or in a tent, try to find level ground that is not subject to water flow from uphill. Look on the ground where you plan to sleep. Do you see evidence of water running through that spot? If so, find another location. Also look for a layer of natural duff, such as leaves or pine needles that indicates water not running through it, as running water will scour the ground. The duff will pad your sleeping zone. Do not clear the ground entirely before setting up your bedroom, but do look for sticks, rocks, and other obstructions that might interrupt your sleep.

If you like to cook over a fire as I do, your kitchen will be located near the fire ring. I will have my grill and stove—if I bring it—located in one general area. My food will be nearby while in camp but if I leave and go fishing it will be hung up.

A backcountry angler traveling on foot will have a spartan living room. This may merely amount to a backpack leaning against a tree with a sleeping pad to sit on. That is one of the reasons I carry a closed-cell sleeping pad, because I can use it when sitting around the fire or camp, and I don't have to worry about it bursting as I do an air mattress. Additional comforts will be found in your camp furniture. Backpackers have to take what they can find in the natural surroundings for their camp furniture. At preestablished sites, you will often find a combination of logs and rocks centered around the fire ring. Sometimes, logs are placed over rocks located at either end, creating a bench of sorts. When looking for a site, consider the camp furniture, not only for yourself, but also your belongings. Satellite boulders and rocks can act as tables for your cook set and other gear you prefer to store off the ground, especially when it rains—water will splatter muck onto gear left on the ground. Also, consider where you will store your rods at the camp. Keep them standing up and out of the way.

The campsite bathroom should be well away from the other parts of camp. When using the bathroom, head away from camp and away from water—which you will be drinking and also where you will be fishing—and find a concealed location. Dig a hole using a stick or the heel of your shoe, preferably six inches deep, do your business, burn your toilet paper, and then cover the hole.

Moving Camp versus Base Camp

Backcountry anglers should consider whether to set up a base camp or keep moving day-to-day. I'm not a fan of refishing waters that I fished the day before. The advantages of setting up base camp are having a fixed campsite, which will free you from the chores of setting up and breaking down camp on a daily basis. This will avail you more fishing time. Preferable locations for a fixed camp will be at the confluence of two or more streams. I have stayed for four days at one campsite simply because the main stream and its tributaries flowed nearby for two anglers to cover over that time within reasonable walking distance. By reasonable walking distance I mean within 3 or fewer miles one-way to reach new waters. When doing this I suggest using regular hiking shoes of choice to get to the waters and changing to your fishing shoes upon arriving at the creek.

The advantage of moving camp on a daily basis is that you will be setting up on fresh water every day. This allows for convenient fishing in the immediate vicinity of where you are staying. You will also get to camp at new locations and that will give you a chance to enjoy more splendor of the backcountry area. If you are going on a long backcountry fishing expedition, I suggest staying at one camp for two nights during the middle of the trip just to free you from the daily making/breaking camp ritual.

Camps by Boat

The four of us were floating Arkansas' Buffalo River. It was our last night of a five-night trip. The river had fallen from its spring high and the fishing improved greatly. The temperatures were in the mid-70s and we were catching smallmouth bass throughout the day. That afternoon, when the sun began to sink below the horizon, we came upon a curve in the river. Across from us rose a spectacular bluff, which overlooked a huge gravel bar with plenty of level spots. The high water had left ample driftwood to warm us in the cool evening. We gently landed the canoes. My brother Mike proclaimed it the perfect campsite, and it was.

Despite the above story, finding a perfect backcountry campsite at the right moment can be as rare as an eclipse. While paddling you are still looking for the basics such as a flat spot and natural amenities to help you deal with the elements at hand, such as wind, sun, etc. You also have additional considerations, such as boat landings and camp fishing.

Finding a campsite from water is not always as easy as it looks. When paddling, you are at the lowest point and always looking up at the land. In some places, such as the Kentucky's Cumberland River, you must get out of your boat and physically look for a suitable campsite. Be prepared to hunt a campsite along sloped and/or wooded shores. After traveling many rivers, patterns where campsites are located become clear. Camping flats can be at the confluence of two streams. Sandbars and gravel bars can often be found on the inside of sharp river bends. Therefore, perusing a map for sharp river bends or the confluence of streams will yield potential campsites.

When looking for a boat landing, look for a moderate slope where you can land your craft. It doesn't have to be perfect, just good enough to hold your boat. You can—and should—always pull up your boat. It had been a hot sunny day of river fishing, so we headed onto a gravel bar a little early, casually throwing up camp, relaxing and consuming cold beverages and telling fish stories. That evening thunder rolled and lightning crackled upriver. Ours was a rainless night. Next morning, I awoke in fog, and stumbled down to the river for coffee water. My canoe was gone. Overnight, the river had risen enough to float the boat away. Our fishing rods and tackle boxes were in there, too. Disaster! Surely if we were lucky enough to find the canoe, it would be overturned, minus our fishing gear. Luckily, we had two boats, and my brother Mike and I sped downriver, sans coffee, looking for the boat. We went over one shoal, then another. No boat. The fog made us worry we would miss the boat entirely, though the river was narrow. Ahead, the canoe! It was lodged into a low hanging tree, facing downstream as if it were guided by paddlers. Our fishing equipment and all gear were intact; only my pride was compromised.

Always pull your boat above the body of water on which you paddle, especially rivers, and especially when thunderstorms are likely. It can rain above where you are and not rain on you, just like in this case, but the river will rise and take away your boat. If I expect a potentially high rise, I'll pull the boat up and tie onto a tree or a tent pole for good measure. Also, when it rains, a boat pulled up to a lake can float away. The lake rises a bit from the rain, and the boat fills with rainwater, which helps it slide to the lake. Add a little wind and presto—no more boat. Also, if rain is predicted, don't leave your fishing gear in the boat, because when the canoe fills with rainwater your tackle box and reels can become soaked.

Gravel bars and beaches make great landings. Also look for the point where a tributary flows into the stream you're floating on. The tributary will form a break in the shoreline, allowing you to get up on the shore to access a campsite.

Sandbars look like great campsites from the water, and they can be. They are unencumbered by vegetation, can be easily leveled without damaging the environment, and generally will have fewer insects. The downside is the sand itself. It can get in your sleeping bag, in your tent, in your food, and just about everywhere else. And when it rains, the sand will stick to everything. I think there's still sand in my left ear from a 16-night backcountry fishing trip in the Everglades a decade ago.

I prefer gravel bars to sandbars. Depending upon the size of the gravel they can have many of the positive traits of a sandbar without all the particles of sand getting on everything. Gravel bars do not provide as good of a sleeping environment as do sandbars, but you can find places that can be leveled and made into better sleeping areas. Always look at the downstream end of a gravel bar, because it will have the smallest granules, hence the best spots to pitch your tent. Gravel bars will also sometimes have trees growing from them to provide shade. You must consider how these bars were formed—from flooding when the water is high. If heavy rain is likely and there is a chance of flooding, do not camp on a gravel bar or sandbar.

Another consideration is camp fishing—being able to fish from camp. It was my nephew's first backcountry fishing trip. He was the only child in the group and wasn't achieving much success on the river, catching more trees than fish. When we pulled into camp that afternoon, Matt was more than a little dejected. I was tossing a spinner into the pool next to camp and pulled out a nice bream. My nephew then grabbed his rod and saddled alongside me as the evening air cooled. He ended up catching five feisty panfish after being skunked the whole day. Around the fire that night, he found his swagger, and his renewed confidence led to his success the rest of the trip, including a 16-inch smallmouth he brought in, despite being simultaneously coached by his father and two uncles. A slow day on the river can be salvaged with some surprise action at camp. When camp fishing, make it a relaxed effort and keep an open mind—you never know what you might catch. Throwing lures will get results but you can only go so far with that. Consider bringing a bobber, sinkers, and hooks to

Camp fishing can be fun and productive, especially for kids.

bait-fish. Or you can "tight-line"—letting your bait sit at the bottom, keeping the line tight, most often casting downstream with the current so you can watch the tip of your rod for nibbles. Use whatever bait is available—hot dogs, bacon, insects, or even some worms you may have brought for such a purpose.

When paddling lakes or coastal areas, you can normally backtrack, tides allowing, if you see a desirable campsite. Coastal campsites will often be beaches or have beaches. Paddle up tidal creeks, looking for high ground. Islands are a good choice whether you are camping along the coast or on lakes. Try to find campsites that suit your daily needs. Say you are backcountry fishing in northern Minnesota in early June. On a typical week-long trip you may need the following campsite characteristics: shade when sunny and hot, shelter from wind when cold, and bug-stopping breezes.

Campsites don't always appear at the precise moment in which we want to start camping. Allow yourself ample time to find a spot, especially if there are other backcountry anglers on the water. Start with expecting Shangri-La and modify your desires. Prepare to lower your expectations as the day gets late. Pick a campsite and stick with it. Sometimes a bad campsite starts looking better after you are settled in. That way you can get some fishing in before dark. Being able to fish from the camp is an important consideration for me. It's always fun to see who is going to get a camp fish.

If at all possible, try not to camp on private land. Different states have different laws regarding navigability of rivers and what is the public domain on a navigable river. Often times the public domain of a navigable river reaches to the high water mark of a given waterway. If you set up camp on private land and are confronted, apologize, break camp and move on. It's better to try to keep good relations with riverside landowners than try to explain that you are below the high water mark, and therefore in the right. When on private property, take extra care to clean up after yourself thus giving landowners no reason to become hostile toward backcountry anglers camping along a stream.

The same advice goes for placing your bedroom, kitchen, living room, and bathroom at a boat-accessible backcountry campsite as it does at a backpack-fishing campsite. The best way to organize your camp is to do it as you unload your gear from the boat. Do this in an organized format that you can use over and over—sleeping gear together, kitchen gear together, fishing gear together, etc. Again be wary of rising water before setting up your tent. You won't have this trouble on lakes. Make your campfire below the high tide line if on the beach, or on gravel or sand if along a river. When using the bathroom, try to get the above the river's high water mark or above the high tide line to allow ample time for decomposition rather than being washed into the water.

One final note: never leave your pole on the ground at camp for any time or for any reason. One time, four of us were paddling down a national park stream so secret I can't even tell you its name. There we were on day two, ready to tackle more remote and fishy waters. We excitedly carried gear from the campsite to the yet-to-be-loaded canoes, where stream waters lapped against their sides. The spring sun revealed a glint on the ground. I looked down. A fly rod lay broken, set on the ground by one of our party and stepped on by who knew? The result was one guy had to watch the others fish.

In the early days of backcountry fishing by boat, I went very minimally, sitting against a tree and cooking on the ground. Nowadays, I go for a little more comfort. Folding camp chairs have come a long way and are dirt cheap. A pair of these makes sitting on a sandbar overlooking a bluff all the more pleasant. Three-legged camp stools store more compactly and can be a good choice if weight and space is a serious concern, such as when portaging or if you are traveling in a sea kayak. I use a cooler as a table, though it has drawbacks. For one, you have to take everything off the cooler to get in it. Secondly, you have to keep your table-cooler away from the campfire, where you may often sit. Plastic storage boxes, used to tote dry food and other goods, make excellent tables, though you will face the same problem as coolers if you have to get into them. Other people bring long planks, stored at the bottom of the boat in transit, and then elevate the planks with storage boxes. These wood tables are advantageous in that you can cook atop them, as opposed to plastic boxes.

What Do I Wear? Or Clothes Make the Angler

What you wear while backcountry fishing may not necessarily help you catch more fish but you might as well be more comfortable while fishing. Below is a list of clothing suggestions for the backcountry angler.

From the Ground Up

Fishing Shoes

Stream-fishing the backcountry by foot means getting your feet wet. Wet feet bring about differing concerns. Concern number one is footing. You aren't going to fish too far if you're slip-sliding up the stream. The obvious solution is felt-soled fishing boots. I don't know what anglers did before these but they sure are an improvement over days gone by. In my early years of fishing, when the cost of a lure nearly broke this broke college student, buying felt-soled shoes was simply cost prohibitive. So I either slogged around in my leather hiking boots, which protected my feet and ankles but didn't prevent slippage, or I wore high-top canvas shoes, which were lightweight but neither protected my feet nor kept traction. I somehow survived that time and now primarily bring along lightweight felt-soled fishing shoes. This is another item where you get what you pay for. I have seen other people glue all-weather carpet to the bottom of their shoes but the carpet comes unglued eventually, usually sooner.

I have to admit, however, that as I've aged and pack weight has become a concern, I have used high-top lightweight hiking shoes for hiking and fishing, such as the Merrell Moab Ventilator. It offers foot support for backpacking and is designed to drain water from the boot. This way I have to carry only one pair of boots.

The second concern is coolness of the water. For warmth, wool socks help a little. Wet feet are one thing, cold feet are another, and fishing with cold, wet feet on a slick stream is yet another. Cold feet become numb feet, which decreases your ability to navigate streams. Felt-soled fishing shoes will come in handy if you're on a slick Appalachian stream, whether the water is cold or merely cool. Now if you're wading New Mexico's Middle Fork Gila River in the summer, odds are you won't be worried about keeping your feet warm. Waders are the answer for some. However, I find them too heavy and cumbersome to take into the backcountry overnight. Day-trippers may find them worthwhile, especially thigh waders. Waders continue to become lighter, more supple, and packable every year.

Day-hiker Footwear. Day hikers will be combining foot travel to the stream or lake with their actual fishing experience. It is likely they will need two pairs of shoes, one pair for on the trail and one pair for the water. When choosing trail shoes, consider the terrain. Is the trail rough and rocky? Is it steep? Or is the trail a smooth, widely graded path? Day hikers can get away with low-top hiking shoes if the trail is easy, though if you don't have strong ankles, go with shoes that give ankle support. If the trail is rough, consider even more support, using shoes with a metal shank in them and a more rugged sole. Once on the water, you'll want to change into your fishing shoes for day trips where weight isn't as much of a consideration. I highly recommend felt-soled high-top boots. They are your insurance policy on the water. You are much less likely to slip while traveling around, can get in better fishing positions, and can gain better traction when positioning yourself to cast. Never, ever wade-fish with sandals on. You are inviting disaster. A broken toe or sliced foot will bring terrible consequences in the backcountry.

Backpacking Footwear. Backpackers may have the biggest dilemma when it comes to shoes. They need boots that will support a fully loaded backpack while hiking, shoes for wade-fishing, and also shoes for hanging around the campsite. Having three pairs of shoes on your person during a backpacking trip can add up to a lot of weight. In order to compromise, you may have to do without the camp shoes, especially if the weather is mild. If you're going to do a lot of hiking or are going on a long trip, I strongly recommend having good trail shoes. On a more moderate trip, you may try to combine your hiking boots as your fishing shoes by using lightweight hiking shoes that drain well. Before making this decision, factor in the slipperiness of the stream through which you will be wading. After all, you came here to go backcountry fishing. On particularly slick streams I will sacrifice weight in other departments and bring my felt-soled fishing shoes. When you're backpacking you literally carry your own weight, so you live with your decisions, for better or worse.

Canoeing Footwear. Temperature dictates your footwear inside a canoe. If it's really cold and you want to make sure to keep your feet dry, rubber boots are the ticket. They make it easier to get in and out of the boat because you can step into the water without getting your feet wet. In moderate conditions, any type of shoe, such as a Top-Sider, can work. However, instead of trying to keep your feet dry, you will try to keep the inside of the canoe dry by using a boat sponge, which is simply a large sponge to sop up water inside the canoe. In warmer weather, sandals are the best choice. These allow you to get your feet wet, are comfortable, won't feel clammy, and offer decent traction. Make sure they have straps both over your foot and behind your heel, in case you have to jump out of the boat quickly in moving water. Leave the flip-flops at home. When going overnight, I suggest bringing a pair of camp shoes, a shoe that covers your entire foot. Keep them in a dry bag. This way you can travel around in the forest to collect wood and have additional foot protection for cold and bugs. Reconsider going with bare feet in a canoe. It was a blistering hot summer trip on Florida's Ochlockonee River; my friend went without shoes or socks for several days. His feet became extremely sunburned and swollen. Another downside of barefootin' it is having to jump out of the boat in an emergency situation, bumping into a log and tipping over, etc.

Kayaking Footwear. When kayaking, your feet will get wet. Consider wearing sandals or water shoes. Try to get sturdy water shoes, since your heels will rub on the bottom of the kayak. A little heel padding goes a long way. If the weather is cold, wear wool socks with your sandals. If traveling overnight dry camp shoes are necessary. Make room for them.

Socks

Backcountry fishers, when traveling overnight, should always bring at least two pairs of socks. If you are on the water, weight is less of a concern, so bring three pairs. By nature we anglers are going to be in and around the water so we are apt to get wet. When wade-fishing, we will be wearing socks directly into the water. You'll want to have an extra pair when you're not fishing, with at least one pair of them thicker wool socks for cold and bugs. Today's wool socks have a blend of other fibers that keep them itch-free, pliant, and durable. I recommend SmartWool socks.

Pants

For anglers, thin yet tightly woven pants are the best. You want pants that will protect you from the sun and the bugs, yet be able to dry out quickly. I often wear long pants while wade-fishing simply for the added protection it gives my legs from brush and such. Because they are then wet, I will either wear them dry or wear them somewhat damp and hang them up near the fire to dry completely. An array of modern materials allows for comfortable yet quick-drying fabrics. Go with natural colors such as khaki, green, or dark blue. This way you can blend in with the surrounding scenery while stalking fish. Obviously, this isn't much of a concern while you're paddling but even then you may get out and wade-fish while on a paddling trip. Speaking of which, I'll often wear long pants even on warm summer days simply because they provide the best protection from the sun.

Convertible pants are also popular with the outdoors set. These comprise long pants and short pants in one; a zipper around each leg in the thigh area lets you remove the lower two-thirds of the pants. These pants save weight, but if they get wet you don't have any other pants into which to change. Always bring a second pair of pants when backcountry fishing by boat. In summer, while backpack-fishing, one pair of short pants and one pair of long pants works.

Shirts

As with other articles of clothing, weather will dictate your shirt choices. At the bare minimum you will want to have a short-sleeve shirt and a long-sleeve, button-up collared shirt that you can layer over it. I prefer shirts with pockets. When out in the fishing backcountry overnight temperatures rise and fall and you need to be prepared for the variations. A button-up shirt has more temperature variability than does a pullover shirt. Wade anglers will want to consider muted colors and patterns that blend in with the surrounding scenery. Many backcountry anglers swear by camouflage. When floating you will need shirts that offer protection from the sun. I prefer a light-colored long-sleeve shirt to keep the rays down and me cooler. Another good choice is the Flats shirt, designed for fishing waters of the Florida Keys. These shirts are very lightweight and have added ventilation.

Outer Layers

In cooler weather or summer backpack-fishing destinations such as the western high country, another layer is in order. Fleece jackets come in a wide array of colors and styles and are a great third layer over a T-shirt and long-sleeve shirt. I recommend zip-up fleece jackets—they're easiest to put on and take off, and they offer the most comfort variation, because you can adjust the zipper to meet your needs. A folded fleece jacket also makes a great pillow. If you're trying to save weight or antici-pate less-cold conditions, consider taking a fleece vest. It has the added benefit of giving you freedom of arm movement while fishing.

Jackets

When on Alaska's Kenai Peninsula, I faced cool, windy, and drizzly con-ditions off and on. I had just received an Arc'teryx rain jacket and pants to test out. By the end of the trip, I was thankful to have this jacket and pant. They kept me warm and dry as I fished, while my fellow anglers stayed in camp more often simply because they had lesser outerwear. The quality of rain jackets has improved immensely over the past two decades. I hate to think about those times of wearing a yellow slicker while floating down the river. Today, primarily due to the improvements of the waterproof breathable fabrics such as those made by GORE-TEX, we can stay dry, com-fortable, and protected from the wind. However, be prepared to pay for this quality. You will thank yourself while in the middle of nowhere getting bombed by precipitation, yet staying amazingly dry. A rain jacket is neces-sary on every backcountry fishing trip. Breathable, good-quality rain jack-ets are so thin now we can wear them while float-fishing on the sultriest, drizzliest summer afternoon. The same lightweight jackets can also keep the weight of pack down when backpack-fishing. In cooler times, consider a thicker rain jacket, especially when river floating, because you don't gen-erate as much energy to keep warm as when you're hiking or backpacking. By all means bring rain pants when float-fishing. I try to have a pair with me at the ready when rain is imminent and just slip them over short pants when the rain does come. They will also protect from the wind while on open water, as will your jacket. While wade-fishing in windy conditions I will wear my rain pants, getting the lower half of them wet. I don't mind because the upper half stays warmer and is less subject to the wind. Also rain pants are built to dry out quickly, so if you think about it they can make good wading pants.

Ponchos are unsuitable for backcountry fishing. When you're stream-fishing, they will get caught in the brush and torn up; plus, they do noth-ing for wind protection. In a boat they have limited value as well. It's hard to cast your rod while wearing a poncho, and it's subject to even more wind on the open water.

One final note: in buggy conditions, you may want to consider a bug jacket. It's made of fine mesh that either pulls over or zips up; it also has a built-in headnet. Some bug jackets come with accompanying bug pants, though I have never worn mine. If the bugs are so troublesome that I need to wear a bug jacket, then I'll go ahead and wear long pants.

Hats

Experienced backcountry anglers know the importance of a hat. Hats protect you from the elements such as sun, rain, heat, and they will keep you warm when it's cold. Specifically speaking, there is no one hat to address every condition; however, you can have a hat for each season. In the summer you will want a wide-brimmed, lightweight hat that offers adequate sun protection yet ventilates as well. For years I have used a Columbia Bora Bora Booney. Made of quick-drying nylon, it has a mesh band for ventilation, weighs mere ounces, and can be smashed into a pack. The only downside is the floppiness of the brim, which can't take high winds. Consider a strong-brimmed hat if you plan to be out on the water in windy conditions. For cooler times you will want a waterproof, GORE-TEX–lined hat, such as the Seattle Sombrero by Outdoor Research.

This angler is thinking about more than her hat while reeling in this feisty smallmouth from a small stream.

No matter what hat you buy, make sure it has a neck strap. This way you can cinch it under your chin during windy conditions or slip it off and let it lay on your back with the strap around your neck when not in use. Also make sure the brim doesn't hang too low or it will get in the way of your vision for casting.

Though not technically a hat, consider a headnet for buggy conditions. A headnet is one of those items that when you don't need it, you have no other use for it, but when you do, you *really* need it. If you are going to be along the backcountry coast, consider a fine mesh headnet to keep out no-see-ums as well as mosquitoes.

Other Items

Gloves

I generally shun gloves, except for in extreme cold. However backcountry anglers may consider paddling gloves, not only for the added comfort in paddling but for sun protection. I find paddling gloves a hindrance while casting, but if you have sensitive skin, consider them. I have seen those open-fingered, wool fishing gloves and figure if it's that cold, you might as well wait until another time to go backcountry fishing. When handling large fish such as those of the saltwater variety as well as pike, a rubberized fish glove makes for a better, safer fishing experience. They are worth their weight in gold when you need them. Try to wash them out frequently, because they'll become quite fishy-smelling. Then after you are done with your backcountry trip, try to dry the gloves out in the sun. A dry fish glove is much less smelly than a wet fish glove. But a sweet-smelling fish glove is worse than anything—it means you haven't caught any fish.

Bandanna

I almost always use a bandanna while in the outback. While backcountry boat fishing I keep one around my neck for added sun protection. Bandannas also come in handy around camp whether you are on foot or boat. They can be used as a towel, potholder, pot cleaner, head wrap for bugs, signal flag, coffee filter, tablecloth, etc.

Eyewear

Sunglasses are protection for the eyes and an important tool for the backcountry fisher. All anglers should invest in sunglasses that not only provide 100 percent UV protection, but are also polarized. Polarized glasses eliminate the reflective glare off the water surface and allow you to see *into* the aqua below. This will help you find fish, see the habitat in which the fish are living, and help you decide the best means to catch fish. By all means bring a neck strap for your sunglasses. This allows you to take them off and not have to worry about losing them or dropping them in the water, and they will always be handy because they are around your neck. Consider bringing some premoistened lens cleaner wipes so you can see your best while backcountry fishing.

Note to older anglers: don't forget the reading glasses; otherwise, tying lures, unhanging knots, and other minutiae will become a nightmare. Without glasses you'll be wrangling with a lure while your buddy will be pulling in the fish. There is another way. Be apprised of magnifiers to help tie on lures. One type clips onto the bill of a cap whereas another style clips onto the top of your sunglasses. Then you simply flip the magnifiers down and presto, you can see to tie on that tiny fly.

Backcountry Camping Gear

Overnight backcountry anglers, whether going on foot or by boat, need sleeping accommodations. There are many choices. Because we have limited space and weight we need to decide exactly what to take to tailor each specific trip.

Shelters

Tents

Tents are the time-honored shelter of choice. But before you run out and load your nylon bubble ask yourself why you are staying in a tent. There are four primary reasons for taking a tent with you on a backcountry fishing trip: bugs, precipitation, cold, and wind. A tent will keep the bugs out, the rain away, make it a little warmer, and will block the wind. However, a tent is an enclosure that keeps you from the place in which you came to see. And they can be hot. If taking a neophyte camper out, I recommend a tent. For some reason tents provide a mental protection from the "unknowns" of the outdoors as well as a physical protection for first-time outdoorspeople.

Backpacking and kayaking anglers will have to consider a smaller tent, sacrificing tent space for weight. Be prepared for close quarters when sharing a tent that weighs under five pounds, but if you are carrying a tent on your back you don't want one that weighs any more. With tents you can drop a pretty penny, but there are also some adequately performing midpriced tents out there, such as those made by Eureka! Stay away from low-end tents found at megastores. They have questionable waterproof ability and limited life span. Canoeists can go for bigger models. These will weigh more but not necessarily cost that much more because oftentimes the smallest tents can be the most expensive, since they are made of pricey lightweight materials.

Screened Shelters

Canoeists can also take along a screened shelter. These are large, 12' x 12' x 7'–high shelters with screened walls and zip-up entries connected to an aluminum frame. They're somewhat bulky, weighing around 20 pounds, but they're great if you're paddling an area with little shade and/or potential insect problems. Such shelters are large enough to cook in, hang out in, even sleep in. They don't have built-in floors, though. I have used the Eureka! Breezeway for years in the Everglades, and it's served me well on the beaches, among other places. For both tents and screen shelters, consider sand stakes when on the beach.

Tarps

Tarps can be used by both backpack and paddling anglers as your primary shelter if not in bug country. I used to carry those big heavy blue tarps way back when. Today's silicone-impregnated tarps can be 10' x 12' and weigh as little as one pound. Because these tarps are so light, try to go for a larger size. This will allow extra room for you and your gear. Tarps can be configured in any variety of ways. If the wind is high and rain is coming, set your tarp low. Otherwise you may consider setting one end low with the other end a little higher, allowing you to get under it more easily. Canoeists can bring along an extra tarp to hang out under during inclement weather, saving their primary shelter exclusively for sleeping, especially if that primary shelter is a tent. With a tarp you can set it up fairly high, bring your camp chairs under the tarp, and be able to relax without having to be inside your tent. When you are inside a tent you invariably lie down and when you lie down you invariably go to sleep. Tarps can be used as sun protection as well when at camp. Bring plenty of cord to string up your tarp—at least 15 feet for each corner to be on the safe side, with a separate 40-foot cord to string a main line between trees.

Backpack anglers have a weight-saving option: a tarp and bug screen combination. Buy a single-person bug screen that weighs mere ounces and combine it with an ultralightweight tarp. I have used this combo on backpack-fishing trips throughout the West. This entire setup is very small, packable, and can weigh less than two pounds. If there is no rain I will set up the bug screen by itself. If rain is a possibility I will set up the bug screen under my tarp. Some of these bug screens are shaped like a coffin, say, 3' x 3' x 6', and have strings coming from each corner for securing the shelter. Other bug shelters have a single string in the middle that ties onto an overhead branch, and then the four corners are staked down.

Sleeping Bag

The primary concerns when choosing a sleeping bag for backcountry angling are warmth, space, and weight. You want a sleeping bag to match the season and situation. For example, you will want a fairly warm sleeping bag on a spring backpack-fishing trip in West Virginia's Cranberry Backcountry, or a summertime Western destination such as Wyoming's Cloud Peak Wilderness. If you're traveling a blackwater stream of the Deep South in the summertime, you want the lightest bag possible.

For all but the warmest times I recommend a sleeping bag comfort rated to around 40°F. These can handle the cold fronts in spring and chilly Rocky Mountain nights without weighing too much. If the temperature dips below this, just put on more clothes and you'll be fine. In warm summertime conditions use a simple zippered fleece blanket, an item you can get cheaply. But beware—you can pay too much by going for a name brand that performs no better than the cheap ones.

Paddlers don't need to worry so much about weight of the sleeping bag but kayakers need to worry about space. Many modern sleeping bags, especially those with down fill, can compress to the size of a water bottle. Canoeists can go more for comfort without having to worry so much about space, unless they are in portaging country. Backcountry anglers

Wyoming's Cloud Peak Wilderness is a fantastic backcountry fishing destination.

generally will not be doing their thing during the depths of cold and don't need to worry so much about extreme condition sleeping bags. Note that for additional comfort you should consider carrying a small camp pillow or bundle your clothes up under your head.

Sleeping Pad

Sleeping pads are every bit as critical to a good night's rest as is a sleeping bag. And a good night's rest is essential for a good day's fishing, so don't overlook your sleeping pad. For good sleeping, I combine a simple closed-cell foam pad, six feet in length, with a lightweight three-quarter-length, 48-inch, self-inflating air mattress on top of it. The lighter model air mattresses come in under a pound each.

A closed-cell foam pad can be used under you while sleeping but also around the campsite and will keep you from popping a hole in your air mattress should you use it lying around camp or by the fire. Canoeists can get extravagant and bring some of the larger-sized air mattresses such as those that are blown up with an electric pump. Those mattresses are quite bulky and can take up significant room in the boat. It seems the older you are, the more elaborate your air mattress gets while backcountry camping.

Backpacks

For the past couple of decades, internal frame packs have supplanted external frame packs in popularity. Sure, there are plenty of external frame backpacks out there, but internal frames rule the roost. Internal packs fit closer to your body and are more compact, whereas external frame packs are generally bigger and bulkier, but have more pockets, which helps organization and loading. Internal pack users have to take more of a "duffel bag" approach to their loading.

For the backcountry angler, which pack you choose is a matter of personal taste. For example, when going off trail or on shorter trips I prefer an internal pack. Conversely, while on a longer trip or a hiking through open terrain I prefer an external pack. Your starting point for choosing a backpack is as simple as fit. Head to your nearest outdoor store and try some on, or borrow a friend's pack. Specialty outdoor retailers often rent packs.

How often do you plan on going backpack-fishing? Name brand packs offer quality and durability. Consider how much gear you like to carry. Do you like to bring everything but the kitchen sink? Or do you carry only the barest of necessities? An overnight backpack should have at least 3,500 cubic inches of space. Imagine where you would put all your gear when looking at a pack. Backpack anglers will generally have more stuff, both in weight and bulk than your average backpacker because you will be carrying a rod, fishing shoes, lures/flies, and perhaps a skillet. Consider where you may store your rod on your pack. Avoid the flimsy, superlight backpacks carried by Appalachian Trail thru-hikers, because they simply will not hold the amount of gear a backpack angler is apt to have. Furthermore, pack weight isn't as much of an issue for backpack-fishers because we are more likely to cover fewer miles on the trail simply because we want to cover waters with our rods instead.

Other Stuff You May Want to Bring Along

Cameras in the Backcountry

How many times have you been backcountry fishing and turned a corner, thinking, "This scene ought to be framed!" Carrying a camera in the backcountry will help solidify your memories and fish pictures will legitimize your angling tales. Digital cameras have the added video feature that can be used to chronicle your wife bringing in her second-best catch. While paddling on the water, simply keep your camera inside its case and inside a personal-sized dry bag. Try to keep the dry bag out of

With a camera you can capture photos, such as this one from Ontario's Quetico Provincial Park.

the sun to keep from overheating your camera. In backpacking backcountry, keep a plastic baggie to put around your camera, put it inside the camera case and then inside another baggie. I'm reluctant to take the camera while wade-fishing streams, since that unexpected slip can have disastrous results. Some anglers will put their camera in waterproof cases, such as those made by Pelican.

Binoculars

Binoculars are not only fun to have when you want to look at something far away but they can actually be useful for the backcountry angler. You can use them for reading channel markers in the saltwater backcountry, watching birds everywhere birds are, looking for campsites in the distance, finding portage trails where they meet the water, and reading rapids ahead, whether you want to see them for their fishing potential or how best to run them.

GPS

Global-positioning systems have come a long way in recent years and have crept into our everyday lives. And they can be of use in the backcountry as well. GPSs are an integral part of my writing hiking and paddling guidebooks. The downloadable nautical maps for saltwater boaters and topographic maps for backcountry anglers help keep you oriented. The saltwater maps show islands, passes, channels, channel markers, and so on, and also display water depths, which can help while paddling through places at low tide and finding fishing locations. Backpack and paddler anglers can use them to count mileage as they travel, and they can mark key waypoints, such as campsites and fishing holes. When I'm backpack-fishing, I'm not so concerned with the miles hiked per day, but rather use it for marking particular locations. I generally do not take the GPS while backcountry fishing by foot—it's just one more thing to drop or lose, and weight is an issue, too. Also, to make the GPS function properly, you need to have it facing upward to the sky, and the absolute best way to do this is hold it in your hand, where you ought to have a fishing rod.

GPSs can be constantly helpful on the water, and they do have waterproof marine models. I turn mine on, after hooking the GPS lanyard to something in the boat, and just let it go. I can check the miles traveled, average speed, average moving speed, amount of time stopped, time of day and more, while keeping up with where I am, and marking fishing hot spots. It is more important to time your river travel than on land. Say you are on a 60-mile five-day paddling trip. You don't want to travel too far in a day and get to the end point too soon, nor do you want to fall too far behind. In this case, a GPS would keep you on average of 12 miles per day. All else being equal, I prefer to stay behind in mileage rather than getting ahead. I can always catch up with a hard day of paddling, but it is hard to lag behind while trying to cover water, sometimes the current just pushes you along.

Another element of the GPS is its ability to give the best hunt/fish times for the area where the GPS is at currently. These hunt/fish tables are based on the movements of the sun and moon, which in turn affect the movements of the earth's water. Fish and game are more active at certain times of the day based on these criteria. Dawn and dusk are major sun-based factors. But it is not simply a matter of following the stages of sunrise and sunset, for the moon factors in as well. This theory, combining the effects of the sun and the moon, was formulated and placed into solunar tables by a fellow named John Alden Knight back in the 1930s.

Not only do these tables give you the good times to hunt and fish, they will have best times, sometimes given as minor and major times, and will tell you if you are going to have an average, poor, or good day. I do take stock in these tables; however, it won't stop me from going back-country fishing when I want to go backcountry fishing. That said, I'm firmly convinced that moon phases affect saltwater fishing more than they do freshwater fishing, simply because the moon affects the tides. (Saltwater fish are more active during higher tides because higher tides cause more water to move. Saltwater fish also feed on a full moon, which makes them feed less during the daytime in a full-moon cycle.)

Weather Radio

A weather radio can be vital in the backcountry. These broadcasts originate from the National Oceanic and Atmospheric Administration (NOAA). The NOAA not only predicts forthcoming weather, upon which you can plan or alter your trip, but it also gives short-term forecasts, which, especially during thunderstorm season, tell you of strong, potentially life-threatening rain, wind, and lightning storms. It will give names of counties and areas in nearby counties, helping you gauge where you are in relation to the storm, and what you should do in reaction to the storm, such as getting off the water if you're paddle-fishing or returning to camp if you're backpack-fishing.

A weather radio also tells sunrise and sunset times. Traditionally, around dusk and dawn are more productive fishing times. Knowing sunset and sunrise can increase your productivity. They also give marine forecasts, when you are near the ocean, including wind speeds and wind direction. These forecasts are absolutely vital to a saltwater paddler. You can adjust your trip to leave early in the morning, or stay off open waters if the winds are high. Tide information is given, too. Fish the tides. This way, you can alter your trip to go with the tide rather than against it. Finally, the weather radio has an alarm, in case you want to get up early to fish.

However, check the weather *before* you leave home. This way you can know what to expect, and also whether to delay or cancel your trip. Furthermore, well before your trip, especially if it is to a far away unknown place, check weather averages, so you can get an idea of what to expect when it comes to temperatures and precipitation. That way you can be well prepared for backcountry conditions.

Backcountry Cooking

So You Want to Cook Your Fish

Cooking your catch adds a touch of self-sufficiency to the backcountry fishing trip. And fresh fish tastes great, too. It's best to decide before you begin your backcountry fishing trip whether you're going to keep your fish or not. From the moment you catch a fish until the moment you cook your fish you have to do something with it. Let's presume you are at the point of catch. You'll have to store the fish until you arrive at camp. If on foot you will likely be using a stringer. If you can't store them live in the stream, (see page 90), then I recommend immediately gutting the fish. This makes the fish lighter to carry and you aren't going to eat the guts anyway. Dispose of the guts in deep or fast moving water. If on a lake, wrap the guts around a rock and throw them far into the lake. Never dispose of guts at a campsite. Fish guts will attract bears and disgust the people coming behind you at the campsite.

After your fish is gutted, string the fish through the thin skin just inside the bottom of its lower lip. Another advantage of gutting the fish immediately is that you can cut its stomach open and see what it has been eating. This way you may adjust your offerings. Remember; never gut a fish unless you are absolutely sure you're going to keep it.

Paddlers have more options. For starters you can string the fish through the lower lip and allow it to stay alive in the water with a stringer attached to the boat. The longer a fish stays alive between catching time and cooking time the better it is. If you have a cooler you can put your fish in it, though the live option is the best one.

How long does a fish stay good? From our modern point of view, it seems a fish would go bad in a matter of minutes. This simply isn't the case, though storage and weather conditions will affect how long a fish stays good. If the fish gills are still red or pink, the fish should be okay to eat; if the gills have turned brown, you may want to reconsider your dining options. You can also press the flesh of the fish. If it's firm, it's okay

119

to eat. If it's mushy, leave it be. Just because a fish has become stiff doesn't mean it's inedible. If a stiff fish passes the above tests, it should be fine.

To Fillet or Not to Fillet

When deciding whether or not to fillet your fish, consider the size and type of fish you have. For example, if you have a small trout you will not have much meat even with the best of fillet jobs. But if you cook the fish whole, you'll have more meat. Keep the skin on—it's tasty and nutritious. If your fish are larger, then you might want to fillet them. Bigger fish not only have more meat, they are easier to fillet simply because they are larger and allow for a little error while moving your knife around. I generally leave the head on smaller trout when cooking. Not only does this allow for more meat to be had in the area between the body and the head, it also allows me something to work with when handling the fish while it is cooking. Before cooking, go over your fish one last time, pulling off anything you don't want to cook or eat, and rinse clean.

How to Fillet a Fish

First get the right knife. A good fillet knife has a long, thin, flexible blade. Do not skimp on quality when it comes to a fillet knife. Keep it sharp. Try to find a smooth, flat cutting surface. Consider a flat streamside rock or piece of wood. A kayak or canoe paddle makes a good cutting board. You may want to avoid this if using expensive ultralight paddles. Lay the fish's head to your left and its stomach away from you. Make the first cut downward, behind the gill cover. Cut only until the knife touches the backbone. Do not cut through it.

Now, run the blade through the fish, parallel to the surface on which you are cleaning, cutting toward the tail with the blade angling slightly downward to keep sliding along the spine. Make long, even strokes and avoid sawing back and forth. Cut deep enough to bounce the knife along the top of the rib cage. When the knife blade no longer contacts the rib cage, push the knife forward through the width of the fish, with the tip coming out on the stomach side of the fish. Continue cutting along the bone until you reach the tail, and then cut through the skin, cutting the fillet off at the tail. A second method is to cut through the rib cage and remove the ribs along with the fillet. An additional step is then required to cut the ribs away from the meat.

Flip the fillet over to remove the skin. Insert the knife in at the tail and cut the meat from the skin. Hold the fillet in position by pressing down on the skin with your thumb. Depending on the fish, you may want to leave

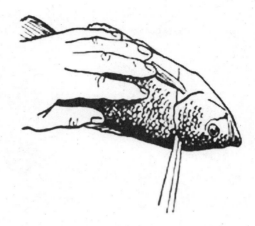

*Make the first cut downward,
behind the gill cover.*

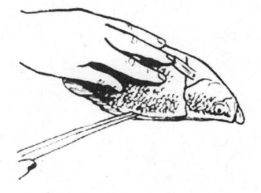

*Run the blade through the fish,
parallel to the surface on which
you are cleaning, cutting toward
the tail with the blade angling
slightly downward to keep sliding
along the spine.*

*When the knife blade no longer
contacts the rib cage, push the knife
forward through the width of the
fish, with the tip coming out on the
stomach side of the fish.*

Continue cutting along the bone until you reach the tail, then cut through the skin, cutting the fillet off at the tail.

Next, flip the fish over and repeat the same steps on the other side.

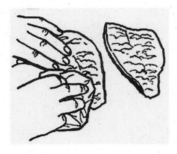

Massage the meat gently to detect other bones.

Flip the fillet over to remove the skin.

Author grills trout over a campfire on Missouri's Eleven Point River.

the skin on if you are going to grill. Skin holds the meat together better. Next, flip the fish over and repeat the same steps on the other side. Now, check for any bones that may remain in the fillet. Slice under whatever bones you see, keeping the blade tight against them to avoid sacrificing any meat, and pull up gently until they detach. Massage the meat gently to detect other bones, using pliers or hemostats for removal. Finally, properly dispose of the fish remains.

Grilling

Fish can be easily grilled whether they're cut into fillets or kept whole. When backpack-fishing, I bring a small, portable 6- by 12-inch grill. Use a larger one when fishing by boat. I build a fire, get some coals up, and place the grill over the coals. Make sure your coals are evenly spread and the grill is sturdy before you put on the fish. Consider keeping a fire on the side of the fire ring in case extra coals are needed to continue cooking your fish. Simply scoot the coals from the adjoining fire under the grill. If you have butter, melt butter and rub it on the inside and outside of the fish before putting it on the grill. This will make it taste better. Add your favorite spices, too. It is almost impossible to keep a fish from sticking to the grates of the grill, though nonstick cook spray can help. Spray it on before you put the grill over the coals. Fish will cook more evenly if you cover them with foil. You can also slow cook fish over the coals with a grill. Use steady but moderate heat, and over time the heat and fumes will cook the fish and give it a smoked taste.

Frying

It was summer, deep in the mountains, under a forest so thick it made midday seem like dawn. This was one of my first solo backcountry fishing trips, so I was actually glad to see other campers at the site when I rolled up. The smell from their campsite drew me over like a moth to a flame. They were frying up fresh trout. The man not cooking invited me over to join in their lunch. The rainbows, rolled in cornmeal and fried to a golden crisp were delicious. It was then and there that I decided to start keeping and eating my own fish. It may seem strange to bring a frying pan with you on a backpack-fishing trip, because weight and space are so important, although there are many lightweight frying pans that are worthy of being carried. For starters get a full-size frying pan, ten inches or more. The small frying pans are just that—too small to cook a fish. Make sure the pan either has a swing-out handle or is handled with a removable pot grabber. A frying pan with a permanent handle is unwieldy in your pack. Choose a pan with a nonstick surface.

Fish can be fried over a fire or over a stove. If you cook over the fire make sure you have adequate coals before you cook. If cooking over the stove, make sure you have enough gas before you start. This way the fish won't be lying dormant in the grease. Have the fish cleaned and within grasping distance before you begin. Cook the fish by themselves, or roll them in cornmeal, pancake mix, or even oats. I prefer using Mexican cornbread meal. It adds a little flavor. Use vegetable oil, olive oil, or butter for cooking. Heat the frying pan with enough oil to cover the bottom half of the fish, or a little less. Gently slide the fish in and let it be. With smaller whole fish, cut the spine in the middle to keep it from curling after it begins to cook. Covering the frying pan with foil cuts down on the mess and more thoroughly cooks the fish. Be patient, and remember that the less you turn the fish, the better. Cook until golden brown. If you want, test one fish to see if it's ready, but remember to account for different-sized fish cooking at different speeds. When all the fish are done, drop them onto a paper towel to drain the oil.

The Old Foil Trick

This is a time-honored cooking method that can result in some scrumptious fare for the patient backcountry fisher. Start with a few feet of foil. Heavy duty foil works best. Break off a piece 12 to 16 inches in length, and then place fish fillet or cleaned whole trout in the foil. Pour in melted butter or squeeze margarine, mix in cut onions, and then throw in spices such as garlic and lemon pepper. Tightly fold the foil so no liquids will escape, adding another layer of foil if necessary.

Once prepared in the foil, the fish can be cooked two ways. First, if you have a grill, set the foil packet on top of the grill, under which lies a deep bed of coals. The alternative method is to place the foil packet directly on the coals. Make sure you have adequate coals before you begin cooking. The upside of using a grill is the ability to keep sliding coals under the grill. It is also less likely to burn the fish inside. But it does cook slower.

This is where patience comes in. Depending on the size of the fish, allow at least 30 minutes before turning the foil packet over. The fewer times you turn the packet, the better. After an hour at least, depending on the size, amount of fish, and amount of coals, take the foil pack off and carefully unfold it. This way, if the fish are underdone, you can put them back on. In my experience, I have almost always underdone the fish rather than overdone them. Enjoy!

Fish on a Stick

When feeling lazy I'll sometimes cook fish on a stick. It requires next to no preparation but you do have to watch a little bit. First, you will need a whole clean and gutted fish. Find any live stick big enough to hold the weight of your chosen fish and long enough to have 12 inches of extra stick beyond the length of the fish. Cut off any outlying twigs, and then insert the narrow end of the stick into the fish from tail to head. Next, force the stick into the ground or set securely with rocks, with the fish leaning over the coals. This takes some time, but that is the beauty of cooking fish on a stick—they cook slower and you really don't have to pay too close attention. They will be tastier if you drip a little butter and spices on them.

Fish can also be added to other dishes, such as fish stew, though I prefer to cook fish on their own, lest other foods taint the freshest of fish—backcountry finned fare caught with your own hand. Great sides for your fish include but are not limited to cornbread, baked potatoes, baked onions, rice, beans, and mashed potatoes.

Sea trout make excellent backcountry fare.

What Other Food Goes in the Backcountry?

People often ask, "What do you eat out there?" Aside from eating the fish I catch, the answer is, "It depends." What type of trip am I going on? How long is the trip? Will I be backpacking? Will I be paddling? The types of food I take will depend on how long I am out. For example, if I am going for a weekend canoe trip down a river, I can bring foods that will fit in a cooler. On the other hand, if I'm going for a 10-night backpack-fishing trip, I will factor weight, space, and shelf life of all the foods I will be carrying. And you can be certain that I won't be carrying a cooler on my back.

Backpack Foods

When you think of backpacking foods, do jerky, gorp, and Ramen noodles automatically come to mind? Or maybe it's freeze-dried weight or stove feasibility? Maybe you just don't care and want to fill your stomach. Care about this: when backpacking, you want foods that have as little water weight as possible, are packaged for travel, are nutritious (or at least filling), and are easy to make. But if you're me, you also think of what you can get away with. Place a grain of salt in your tackle box when you read this and don't blame me for food poisoning.

When I started backpacking in the Smokies, I tried freeze-dried and other prepackaged "add water and wait" meals. Generally coming in foil pouches to which you add boiling water, freeze-dried meals are much tastier than they used to be. This more-expensive-than-average backcountry fare can be found at specialty outdoor stores or on the Internet. After questioning my pocketbook, I started to experiment a bit, bringing my indoor pantry outdoors. I don't have a complete red-capped mini–spice rack or a tiny cutting board to lug around, but I do have some innovative ideas to share.

First of all, why the paranoia about spoiled food? If it smells bad, don't eat it. It's okay. I am guilty of it too at times, but bacteria rapidly multiply below 40°F and above 140°F. The majority of anglers I know backpack-fish for no longer than a week on the average, if not just a few days. So why eat like an Appalachian Trail thru-hiker?

Breakfast. Simple oatmeal is about as dry as you can get, and it's cheap. I recommend the traditional long-cooking oats because they taste better and are more nutritious than the instant kind. I add raisins to my oatmeal to give it a little flavor and add some fruit to my wilderness diet. Raisins are a great example of a dried item with lots of nutrition shriveled up in them. Other lightweight breakfasts include country ham, bagels, and cream cheese. Carry fresh fruit for your first morning, even if it weighs down your pack. If you have a skillet, bring eggs. Then you can make French toast, eggs any way you like them, and even sausage. Look in the frozen food section for precooked, plastic sealed patty sausage. Pancakes are a time-honored camping food, and prepackaged pancake mix is lightweight—it's the syrup that's heavy.

The base of my lunches: flat flour tortillas. Think of tortillas as pre-smashed bread. Other packable breads are bagels, English muffins, and pita bread. Nowadays, tortillas come in varieties such as whole wheat or spinach. I will add peanut butter and fruit preserves (not mere jelly, which is flavored sugar) to make a roll-up sandwich. You have to work to get fruit into your outback diet. Other alternatives are honey or raisins with peanut butter as the base. Tortillas can also be used in lieu of crack-ers. Top them with anything you would a cracker. Put in smoked oysters and add some slices of mozzarella (I prefer pepper jack) and roll up into a nice, greasy, filling lunch.

To meat or not to meat? (If you're vegetarian, skip the next two para-graphs.) Even on the trail, my first night's fare features heavy perisha-bles to cook over hot coals, such as hamburgers with all the trimmings, boneless chicken, or steak and whole baked potatoes or baked onions. Microwave the taters or onions at home, wrap them in foil after smearing them with butter and spices, and all you need is a reheat. Make sure you have a good enough knife for steak, though. If you are paranoid about meat going bad do this: Freeze it at home, wrap it in foil, and it will be thawed by the time you arrive at the first campsite.

Beyond that, meat is good protein and a complete companion to noodles or instant mashed potatoes. Spam and Vienna sausages are a no-brainer, so let's skip to hot dogs, kielbasa, and other precooked links. You'd think that kielbasa and dogs are for the first or second night, but those things will keep for up to a week. Salami and summer sausages are good choices that don't require refrigeration. Get whole rolls and not presliced.

Speaking of what goes good with salami, let's talk about cheese. My tests show that cream cheese keeps well without refrigeration. In fact, regular cheese keeps pretty well, too. It might get a little greasy or malformed in warmer weather, but it neither scares me nor makes me sick. Parmesan cheese keeps great and you can enhance your other meals with it. String cheese and wax-covered cheeses are popular.

Other good snacks include dried fruit, nuts such as peanuts and pistachios, hummus, and sardines with crackers. Don't forget the bars, whether they be candy, granola, nutrition, or energy. Fig bars are a somewhat-healthful choice.

Flour can be versatile if you are willing to transport it. On a four-plus day trip, I will take proportioned flour, baking soda, salt, and dried milk (using the latter to cream coffee). I can make pancakes with the flour, soda, salt, and dried milk. If I take away the soda and add garlic powder and Parmesan cheese, I have Alfredo sauce to go with my noodles. You can use the flour to batter the fish, too. Always mix cold water into your dried milk. It reconstitutes better that way.

Backpackers can carry easy dinners, the standards that can be side dishes to complement fish. They are all lightweight and relatively easy to fix. And if the fish don't cooperate you can still have something to eat. Consider macaroni and cheese, instant mashed potatoes, couscous, stuffing, rice, Ramen noodles (or "remain" noodles, since they remain in your pack until all else is gone).

Other standards, such as jerky and dried fruit, are standards for a reason. They work. They're light. The most important thing is the fishing trip and your backcountry experiences. Develop your own style in everything that you do. There's no reason you can't enjoy what you normally eat, and even look to it as a reward at the end of a hard day. After all, "an army travels on its stomach," so the saying goes . . . and so does a backcountry angler.

Foods by Canoe or Kayak

Pretty much anything you can take backpacking you can take canoeing. Kayakers have to find some sort of middle ground. You may bring a small cooler with you enabling some added possibilities, but your limited room will force you to shop like a backpacker. Try to cull from both a backpacker's and canoeist's menu. For the canoeist with a good cooler you can merely move the contents of your refrigerator to the ice chest. Things that rot quickly need a cooler, so here come the veggies and fruits (I am not big on lemons for my fresh fish, but most go for the squeeze). Baggies full of marinated salad make for a nice cool lunch in the summer. Take some skewers along and have veggie shish kebabs over the fire next to your fish. If you keep the ice clean, add cubes to your favorite soda. Believe it or not, backcountry paddlers with coolers have been known to bring beer with them.

Even when canoeing I will bring flour tortillas for bread. It's what goes inside that changes. I will come up with every form of meat and cheese combination, and maybe slice in some tomatoes. Premade chicken salad, tuna salad, and pimento cheese are also easy choices and make for a fast gravel-bar lunch.

Dinners are limited only by your imagination and your desire to cook. Remember, a long day of fishing on the water will sometimes leave you looking for the easiest possibilities. Rainstorms, unexpected long paddles, and other surprises may also necessitate an uncomplicated dinner. Always have at least one night's meal be an easy one. Look in the deli section of your local supermarket and see what premade dinners are available. If you can cram it into the cooler, it can be yours. When I don't feel like cooking on the first night, fried chicken with slaw on the side is an easy choice.

Foods While Day-tripping

Think pocket lunches. Tortilla roll-ups, as discussed previously, can be hauled around in a light backpack or fishing vest pocket. Anything your mother packed you for lunch in the brown bag will work: Jell-O cups, Fruit Roll-Ups, grapes, an apple, or a warm thermos of soup. Leftovers from home are also a good choice. Keep it simple and then you can focus on catching the big one.

About Water in the Backcountry

You have to drink, whether you are in the backcountry or not. While in the backcountry, especially on long trips, we cannot bring all the water we will need to drink (saltwater backcountry excepted, where we must bring all our freshwater with us because there is no other available). That means we will have to obtain water from the backcountry. I am in the minority, but I drink the water directly from the source and don't treat it. But you may consider the following do-as-I-say-not-as-I-do advice: treat your water. Two of us were backpack-fishing near Yellowstone's Heart Lake for several days. We drank the water directly from the area streams and lakes. My fishing partner got sick from the water and I didn't. The same thing happened while backpack-fishing in Michigan's Ottawa National Forest. Treating your water has become a lot easier these days, but let's harken back for a moment. The old method was to boil your water for at least a minute—there's nothing like hot water to sate a big thirst, plus you have to wait until after your water is boiled, which means you have to have made a fire or broken out your stove. Then came the pump filters. These were once bulky but are now smaller and are still used by a declining number of backcountry visitors. Nowadays people use chemical treatments. Iodine was the choice of days gone by, but has an awful taste and gives you iodine breath, which ain't good. Nowadays we have products like Aqua Mira, where you mix two drops of chemicals together, making chlorine dioxide, wait 30 minutes, and your water is fine. This is the lightest option. And the easier option is to buy a water bottle with a built-in filter. You simply fill your water bottle then suck through a straw, which forces the water through a built-in small filter. These filters need to be replaced but they are a good choice. Another option is the UV filter, which uses ultraviolet rays to kill the bad things in the aqua. Such filters use batteries, which can be problematic if they die. No matter your choice of filters, filtering your water is the safest choice. When backcountry cooking, go ahead and use "raw" water if you are going to boil it anyway, say for macaroni and cheese or coffee. Otherwise treat it and you'll be able to spend your time fishing instead of being sick.

General Cooking Considerations

Now that we know what we are going to cook, what are we going to use to cook it? Backpack anglers once again must factor weight and space most judiciously. My pack always contains a small grill, an aluminum pot that I don't mind putting over the fire, a pot grabber, a Swiss Army knife, and a spoon, plus a frying pan when keeping and cooking fish. Don't forget the spatula; small backpacker-sized models are available. If two or more of you are going on the trip, then y'all can split the cooking items: one takes the grill, the other takes the frying pan, and each of you has your own pot. Aluminum pie tins make for great lightweight and reusable plates. The possibilities expand when you're backpack-fishing by boat. I bring a bigger grill and always bring a stove, whereas on the trail I usually cook over the fire and leave the stove at home.

What Cooking Utensil Should I Bring?

Cook Kit. Cook kits come in a wide variety of sizes and weights, from the nearly weightless titanium sets to sets so big and bulky they belong on a wagon train. Just make sure you have enough pots, plates, and cups for everyone on the trip. Also remember you will be handling hot stuff so have a plan, whether it is bringing pot grabbers, using bandannas or a chef mitt. I like to also bring paper plates so I can just burn them after eating.

Grill. Have a grill big enough to cook your fish and other goodies for everyone in the party. Visualize how you will be using a grill. Will you be setting it up with rocks? Does it have legs? Don't wait until you are about to throw on the bass fillets to figure out how to set your grill over the fire.

Frying Pan. Frying pans can be used for more than just fish. They can be used to sauté vegetables, stir-fry rice, make quesadillas, and of course make breakfast. If the pan comes with a pot grabber, by all means bring it along. Pans with built-in handles are acceptable when fishing by canoe.

Cup. Plastic cups, such as stadium cups, are best. They are durable enough, can be used for hot or cold drinks, and can hold large amounts. Most coffee cups and mugs are too small. Insulated cups are good for winter, but in milder weather end up keeping your coffee too hot for too long. No glass in the backcountry.

Utensils. The spoon is the most versatile utensil in the backcountry. It can do almost anything a fork can, yet a fork cannot quite do what a spoon can. That must be why they invented what is known as a spork, which basically looks like a spoon except it has tines on the front. Another possibility is an all-in-one utensil, which folds out from a knife body—spoon and fork and knife. But they all end up being too short to dig deep into a pot, and you invariably get food onto the knife body.

Stove versus Fire. Maybe I'm a throwback, but I enjoy cooking over a fire. But for other purposes a stove can more efficient and regulatable. The fire cook has to contend with a fire that can be too hot, not hot enough—insuring uneven heat resulting in smoke in the eyes, blackened pots, burned fingers and an angry chef—if the cook can get a fire going. Stoves are not as subject to rain and wind or cold as fires. But you must bring adequate fuel. However, there is a certain romance and skill to firecraft. It certainly is a lot more fun to sit in front of a fire mesmerized by the dancing flames, rather than listening to the dull roar of a camp stove. Campfire considerations: gather dead and downed wood. It's easier to gather and burns better than live wood. Build fires below flood line on rivers and below high tide line in salty backcountry. Use already established fire rings, whether they are a pile of stones at a streamside flat, or a preestablished steel grate such as those in the Boundary Waters. Before making a fire be aware that use of fire pans are required on some Western rivers. For that matter, get up-to-date on fire regulations before you go anywhere.

Don't be afraid to alter a rock fire-ring. Make it small and rectangular. A rectangular ring is better than the traditional but impractical circle. If campers sit in a circular arrangement around the fire, someone is going to be punished with smoke, unless it blows straight above the fire, which rarely happens. Campers end up sitting on one side of the fire anyway, to avoid smoke. So in arranging the fire ring in a rectangular shape you facilitate the laying of wood on the fire, which, when broken up, is laid best in a crisscross pattern to allow the fire optimum oxygen. Campers sit alongside the fire out of the smoke instead of around it in the smoke. If along a valley stream or river sit either facing the waterway or your back to the waterway. For smoke goes upstream by day and downstream by night, following the winds.

Stoves. Like all other backcountry camping gear, stoves have become smaller and more efficient over the years. Gas stoves, using Coleman Fuel, are the most popular. You have two basic types of gas stoves: a single burner unit with built-in windscreen and gas tank, or collapsible separate stove unit that attaches to a refillable gas bottle. A third type of stove that semi-fits into this category is the liquefied-gas stove. A small collapsible burner attaches easily to a metal cartridge, commonly of butane or propane. Of these three I prefer the single burner with the built-in gas tank. It stays together in one piece and is thus more durable, and durability is what I look for in backcountry gear. The stove that attaches to a refillable gas bottle has too many pieces, and I don't like putting it together and taking it apart every time I use it. The downfall of cartridge stoves is the cartridges themselves. Once it's opened, it's hard to tell exactly how much fuel is in a cartridge, so you always have to carry an extra cartridge. And cartridge disposal is a problem. I'm sure it's not you, and I know it's not me, but somebody is leaving empty cartridges in the fishing backcountry. Some paddlers bring those big ol' two burner stoves often associated with car camping. These work for large groups.

Alcohol stoves are gaining favor. Primarily used by long-distance hikers, the stoves use denatured alcohol. There is no control over the flame, which is not that powerful even when the heat is concentrated with a windscreen. It would take forever to cook fish with, but it is adequate for boiling water. These small stoves will also run on solid fuel tablets, which deliver about the same results. An alcohol stove can be a good backup if you are planning to cook exclusively over the fire and weather conditions make a fire temporarily prohibitive.

Backcountry Fishing Safety

Throughout this book, safety issues within the various categories of backcountry fishing have been addressed. However, the following is a list of other safety topics that should be considered before you embark into the outback.

Lightning

The summer day started bright and clouded over as the afternoon heat wore on. We could hear thunder somewhere in the distance but were deep in the valley as we floated downriver. What could we do but get our rain jackets out and just wait? And the rain came in torrents, followed shortly by sharp crackles of lightning and wind so strong it was downing branches from trees. We paddled frantically and finally came upon a high vertical bank with a gravel bar below it. We hastily landed and stood with our backs to the high bank, shuddering with every crackle and flash of the ensuing bolts. Lightning can strike a backcountry angler, and with fatal results. Think about it: you are standing in water or floating on water with a fishing pole, aka lightning rod, pointed skyward. Play it smart. When you sense a storm coming have a plan for what you will do when it hits. Most plans will involve getting the hell off the water. Seek shelter in a low area or in a grove of trees, not against a single tree, and wait it out.

Poisonous Plants

You know the adage: leaves of three, leave it be, etc. If you are allergic to poisonous plants, check ahead for the area in which you will be backcountry fishing and take the appropriate action, such as carrying along antihistamine-based creams like Benadryl.

Bugs

Sometimes when backcountry fishing we consider the possibility of death by blood loss from mosquitoes, but actually your chances of dying from a bug bite in the wilds are less than your chances of dying on the car ride to the fishing venue. Watch out for black widow spiders, ticks with Lyme disease (though you can't tell the ones with Lyme disease until you get it). A real danger is from bee stings to those who are allergic to them. You know who you are, so make sure you have some Benadryl in the backcountry.

Bears

Backcountry fishing naturally takes us to more remote areas, where bears are more likely to roam. With this in mind, we have to store our food away from them, where they can't access our grub while we're away fishing. This not only makes our backcountry trip viable and safe, it keeps wild bears wild. I've been places where bear food storage setups have been available at campsites, such as British Columbia's Bowron Lakes Provincial Park, where ladders let you climb to safe storage on horizontal ladders suspended between trees. In the Smokies, a system of cables and pulleys keeps food out of reach. Secured ground level food boxes are used in the Chugach National Forest of Alaska. But don't count on food storage facilities waiting at camp. It is up to us to store our food properly.

While paddle-fishing, you will be with your food most of the time because your food will be in the boat and at the camp with you. But backcountry hikers will inherently leave their camp—and food—to go fishing. I still remember eastern Arizona's Blue River, returning with a stringer full of trout to find my backpack gone, missing from the campsite where I left it leaning on a Ponderosa pine tree. I looked around and there sat a blond-haired black bear, annihilating my pack and food. I went after him shouting (maybe not the best idea, but I was in a dander because a brand new camera was strapped to the pack) and he ran off. My fishing trip was over and the bear got a good taste of the irresistible nectar known as human food.

While in the backcountry, bring enough cord to store your food at least ten feet off the ground, higher in grizzly country, and at least six feet from trees. Simply tie a rock to the line and throw it over the crook of tree A, and then throw the line over the crook of tree B, approximately 15 feet or more from the first tree, stringing a horizontal line. Make it taut. Then, with a second line, tie a rock and throw the second line over the horizontal line. Tie your food sack, hopefully a waterproof one, to the second line, hoisting it off the ground. Tie the unused end of the line to a tree trunk. It's easier said than done but with practice you can do it. A second method is known as counterbalancing. Here, you either tie the horizontal line or find a far reaching horizontal limb well away—six or more feet from the trunk—and at least 15 feet high, and then throw a line over using the rock method. Tie a food bag on, with a loop knot near the bag, and then tie a second food bag on the other end of the rope (or a rock if you don't have enough food). Then, push your food bag up with a long stick till both bags are at least 10 feet off the ground. Obviously, the length of the rope has to be right, and this may take a few tries to get it done correctly. Another time to be bear aware is when you are carrying a stringer of fish down the trail back to camp. I walked with purpose and listened as closely as possible, while toting my stringers back to camp on the Gallatin River in Yellowstone National Park.

Snakes

Backcountry anglers will see snakes in freshwater areas, especially rivers. Some snakes prefer being near the water, and you may have to watch out for snakes, especially on sunny streamside rocks. This is a preferred area for copperheads. I have seen other snakes swimming while floating by in a boat. One snake, while caught swimming in the middle of a big lake, was so tired it tried to get in the canoe. While stream-fishing, which you will likely be doing alone, watch where you are going. Make every step count, whether it is to watch out for snakes or keep from slipping, where remoteness and noise of the stream will keep you from successfully hollering for help, even if someone knew you were injured.

Yellowstone's Gallatin River valley offers backcountry fishing in grizzly country.

Alligators

This hazard is primarily confined to Florida rivers and some blackwater streams and swamps of the Southeast United States from the Carolinas to Texas. Truthfully, though, alligators won't present that great of a danger. However, be aware that gators used to being around fishing folk have been known to go after a hooked fish. This happened to us in Georgia's Okefenokee Swamp. We were swamp neophytes. My friend had caught a bowfin—a type of gar—not knowing what it was at the time. Just then a gator starts coming from the swamp edge right for the line, being well versed at getting hooked fish from anglers. My friend quickly reeled in the fish with the gator in pursuit, and then sticks his hand in the fish's mouth to get it out of the water just before the gator got it. And he quickly found out how toothy a bowfin can be. Meanwhile, as my friend blurted a few unprintable words after tossing the bowfin back in the water and examining his punctured hand, the gator slunk back under the water, to await the next angler.

Sun

When backcountry fishing, the sun can be your enemy and your friend. You welcome it every morning as it warms the camp and lights the world. Then it tries to burn your skin, penetrate your eyes, and kick up gusty winds. Finally you lament its departure every night as darkness falls. Sun can be a real threat no matter where you are. By nature, especially while boating, anglers will be on the water, and thus open to the prowess of old Sol. Be prepared for sun. Have sunscreen, a hat, bandanna, long pants, and a long-sleeve shirt. Clothes are your best defense. Put on the sunscreen before you get in the sun. Consider covering your hands. I have personally seen several cases of sun poisoning on angler's hands, from pale skinned neophytes who figured their hands wouldn't be affected, but if you think about it, while fishing and paddling your hands and arms are outstretched and soaking up the sun, even if they are moving much of the time. One of my worst sunburns was on my arms after a few days of fishing meadows in Yellowstone National Park.

Heat

Heat is normally associated with the sun. Heat problems are likely to occur while fishing by canoe/kayak or while backpacking to a fishing destination on really hot days. While paddling, take shade breaks and swim to cool off in the heat of summer. If you're hiking, try to travel in

Put on sunscreen before you get in the sun.

the cool of the morn or take breaks along the way. The fish can wait, but not too long.

Cold

As an outdoor writer who spends much time in the wilds people often ask me, "When is the coldest you have ever been?" My surprising answer, "Trout-fishing in the spring." In our eagerness to hit the river, especially after a string of nice March days, we take off for the nearest trout stream, disregarding the fact that 21 days of March are classified as winter, and the streams can be really cold then. A day of wade-fishing the backcountry with air temperatures in the 50s and water temperatures below that will numb your feet and slowly work their way up your body. The possibility of hypothermia is very real here. Try to limit your time in the water and break your fishing sessions into shorter, smaller tracts of time. And falling into a stream while fording with a fully loaded backpack can have disastrous ramifications. Mountain areas out West and the lakes of the North Country can turn bone chilling cold no matter what time of year, especially during and after moisture-bearing fronts. I've been snowed on while backpack-fishing Ole Creek in Montana's Glacier National Park during August. On Fish Creek (yes, Fish Creek, I had to go there) in Idaho a hailstorm turned a 90-degree scorcher into a 50-degree bone-chiller in a matter of minutes. While paddling, thunderstorms can turn a hot day into a cold one before you know it. Try to stay dry if possible—it's easier to stay dry and warm, or even dry and not so warm, than to get wet and cold and then warm up.

Medical Kit

Medical kits have come a long way. Now you can find activity-specific medical kits that come in different sizes for each activity—for example, for everything from backpacking to adventure racing. Medical kits designed for water sports come in waterproof pouches. I recommend Adventure Medical Kits, because they hey make a good variety of kits and also divide their kits into group-sized units for backcountry fishers who want to take what they need and no more. So whether you are a solo backpack angler or on a multiple-boat, multiple-day river trip, you will have not only the right kit but the right-sized one.

Where to Go Backcountry Fishing

Planning Your Backcountry Fishing Trip

Before you hit the water, get together with the fellow members of your party to plan your trip. You will want to go over the practicalities of the trip such as who, what, where, when, and how. You also need to go over gear, especially gear to be shared by the group, whether it's the boats, cooking items, or tents. You'll also need to figure out who's going to drive and the means by which you'll be getting to your destination.

When getting a group together, consider the following things: group size, group dynamics, and trip expectations. The more people in a party, the more complicated things become. It's best to keep your group small to give everyone the best fishing opportunities. I prefer to keep backpack-fishing groups no bigger than four people. You may not want to mix your hard partying old college roommate with the deacon at church.

Trip expectations are important. Everyone needs to be on the same wavelength as to what the trip will be like. For example, does everyone want to fish hard all day long and spend very little time at the campsites? Or do they want to spend more time telling fishing tales by the fire than actually fishing? Is everyone willing to go for all ten nights, or will someone want to leave early? Make sure everyone is in agreement about the style of fishing trip. Also, make it clear up front about sharing expenses, chores, and other duties. This way there will be no unpleasant surprises when it comes time to collect money—or wood.

Suggested Backcountry Fishing Destinations: State by State

The following is a list of backcountry fishing destinations for each state. They include hiking and paddling destinations. It covers the bodies of water to be fished, where the waters are, the fish to be caught, backcountry accesses, what maps will be helpful, what types of overnight camping possibilities while fishing, and a helpful Internet information link to get you started. A final comment gives you an idea of what to expect.

Alabama

The Water:	Shoal Creek and small lakes where the creek is dammed
Where:	Shoal Creek Ranger District, Talladega National Forest
The Fish:	Smallmouth and rock bass, bream
Access:	Pinhoti Trail
Maps:	Talladega National Forest
Overnight Possibilities:	Yes, backpacking
Information Link:	**www.fs.fed.us/r8/Alabama**
Comments:	Shoal Creek is clear and beautiful and deep in the forest, has trail shelters as well.

The Water:	Sipsey Fork
Where:	Sipsey Wilderness
The Fish:	Smallmouth and rock bass, bream
Access:	Moulton, Alabama
Maps:	Sipsey Wilderness Trails
Overnight Possibilities:	Yes, backpacking
Information Link:	**www.sipseywilderness.org**
Comments:	It will be tough for the fish to outdo the scenery.

Other potential Alabama destinations: Mobile Tensaw Delta, Cheaha Creek, Choctawhatchee River

Alaska

The Water:	Juneau Creek
Where:	Chugach National Forest
The Fish:	Dolly Varden, rainbow trout, Arctic grayling
Access:	Resurrection Pass Trail
Maps:	Chugach National Forest
Overnight Possibilities:	Yes, backpacking
Information Link:	**www.fs.fed.us/r10/chugach**
Comments:	Well-maintained trail travels along Juneau Creek and lakes, which also offer fishing. Designated backcountry campsites have bear-proof storage boxes.

The Water:	Glacier Bay and freshwater tributaries
Where:	Glacier Bay National Park and Preserve
The Fish:	Halibut, salmon, lingcod
Access:	By kayak
Maps:	Glacier Bay National Park
Overnight Possibilities:	Yes, oceanside camping

Information Link: **www.nps.gov/glba**
  Comments: Kayak tripping here requires extensive planning but can reap trip-of-a-lifetime rewards.

Other potential Alaska destinations: Gates of the Arctic Wilderness, Wood River at Wood-Tikchik State Park, American Creek

Arizona

 The Water: Blue River and tributaries
  Where: Blue Range Wilderness and Primitive Area
 The Fish: Various trout
  Access: Alpine, Arizona
  Maps: Blue Range Wilderness and Primitive Area
 Overnight
 Possibilities: Yes, backpacking
Information Link: **www.fs.fed.us/r3/asnf**
 Comments: At more than 170,000 acres, there is plenty of room to roam and fish.

 The Water: West Clear Creek and tributaries
  Where: West Clear Creek Wilderness, Coconino National Forest
 The Fish: Rainbow and brown trout, smallmouth bass
  Access: West Clear Creek Trail
  Maps: Coconino National Forest
 Overnight
 Possibilities: Yes, backpacking
Information Link: **www.fs.fed.us/r3/coconino**
 Comments: Long narrow wilderness in deep canyon with trails that require wading.

Other potential Arizona destinations: Wet Beaver Creek Wilderness, upper Verde River, Chevelon Creek

Arkansas

 The Water: Buffalo River
  Where: North central Arkansas
 The Fish: Smallmouth bass, redeye, panfish
  Access: Marshall, Arkansas
  Maps: Buffalo National River
 Overnight
 Possibilities: Yes, canoe camping and backpacking
Information Link: **www.nps.gov/buff**
 Comments: America's first national river is managed for backcountry recreation, including fishing, floating, and hiking.

Backcountry Fishing

The Water: Caney Creek
Where: Caney Creek Wilderness, Ouachita National Forest
The Fish: Smallmouth bass, redeye, bream
Access: Caney Creek Trail
Maps: Caney Creek Wilderness Trails
Overnight
Possibilities: Yes, backpacking
Information Link: **www.fs.fed.us/r8/Ouachita**
Comments: Caney Creek crosses Cossatot River, which also offers fishing, before reaching Caney Creek Wilderness. Good smallmouth wade-fishing in pools.

Other potential Arkansas destinations: Kings River, Caddo River, Richland Creek

California

The Water: Tuolumne River and tributaries
Where: Yosemite National Park
The Fish: Rainbow, brown, and brook trout
Access: Tuolumne Meadows
Maps: Yosemite National Park
Overnight
Possibilities: Yes, backpacking
Information Link: **www.nps.gov/yose**
Comments: The park streams and lakes have fish aplenty. Many are underfished.

The Water: Kern River
Where: Sequoia–Kings Canyon National Park
The Fish: Rainbow, brown, and brook trout
Access: Three Rivers, California
Maps: Sequoia-Kings Canyon National Park
Overnight
Possibilities: Yes, backpacking
Information Link: **www.nps.gov/seki**
Comments: Kern River Canyon offers majestic scenery to go along with your angling. Many other streams in park.

Other potential California destinations: Golden Trout Wilderness, Emigrant Wilderness, San Gabriel Wilderness

Colorado

The Water: White River
Where: Flat Tops Wilderness

The Fish:	Cutthroat, rainbow, brown, and brook trout
Access:	Glenwood Springs, Colorado
Maps:	White River National Forest
Overnight Possibilities:	Yes, backpacking
Information Link:	**www.fs.fed.us/r2/whiteriver**
Comments:	Fish both the White River and the high-country lakes atop the White River Plateau.

The Water:	Ouzel Creek and adjacent lakes
Where:	Rocky Mountain National Park
The Fish:	Cutthroat, rainbow, brown, and brook trout
Access:	Wild Basin trailhead
Maps:	Rocky Mountain National Park
Overnight Possibilities:	Yes, backpacking
Information Link:	**www.nps.gov/romo**
Comments:	Numerous trails in park travel along fishing destinations. Be especially aware of stream and lake regulations.

Other potential Colorado destinations: Rawah Wilderness, South San Juan Wilderness, Black Canyon of the Gunnison National Park

Connecticut

The Water:	Housatonic River
Where:	Western Connecticut
The Fish:	Brown trout, pike, smallmouth bass
Access:	Appalachian Trail
Maps:	Appalachian Trail Massachusetts/Connecticut
Overnight Possibilities:	Yes, backpacking
Information Link:	**www.appalachiantrail.org/connecticut**
Comments:	Rural setting with nearby roads but AT does provide venue for fishing here.

The Water:	Various brooks and ponds
Where:	Pachaug State Forest
The Fish:	Cutthroat, rainbow, brown, and brook trout
Access:	Hopeville, Connecticut
Maps:	Pachaug State Forest
Overnight Possibilities:	Yes, auto camping and backpacking with permit
Information Link:	**www.ct.gov/dep**
Comments:	Limited backcountry opportunities.

*Author with bass on
Blackwater River, Florida*

Florida

The Water:	Gulf of Mexico and adjacent tidal waterways
Where:	Everglades National Park
The Fish:	Snook, sea trout, redfish, snapper
Access:	Everglades City and Flamingo, Florida
Maps:	Everglades National Park and nautical charts
Overnight Possibilities:	Yes, by kayak or canoe
Information Link:	**www.nps.gov/ever**
Comments:	Has a lifetime's worth of water, fish half the size of your boat, and 100 miles of wild coastline.

The Water:	Ochlockonee River
Where:	Apalachicola National Forest
The Fish:	Largemouth bass, panfish
Access:	Bloxham, Florida
Maps:	Apalachicola National Forest
Overnight Possibilities:	Yes, canoe camping
Information Link:	**www.fs.fed.us/r8/florida**
Comments:	Great backcountry destination. Can go from near Tallahassee all the way to tidal water in Gulf.

Other potential Florida destinations: Blackwater River, St. Marys River, Suwannee River, Ocklawaha River

Georgia

The Water: Jacks River, Conasauga River, and their tributaries
Where: Cohutta Wilderness
The Fish: Brown and rainbow trout, smallmouth bass, panfish
Access: Chatsworth, Georgia
Maps: Cohutta Wilderness
Overnight Possibilities: Yes, backpacking
Information Link: **www.fs.fed.us/conf**
Comments: Great combination of backpacking and backcountry fishing.

The Water: Upper Flint River
Where: West central Georgia
The Fish: Shoal bass, panfish
Access: Thomaston, Georgia
Maps: Georgia Gazetteer
Overnight Possibilities: Yes, canoe camping
Information Link: georgiawildlife.dnr.state.ga.us
Comments: Flint is a long touring river. Try the Sprewell Bluff area.

Other potential Georgia destinations: Satilla River, Okefenokee Swamp, Chattooga River

Idaho

The Water: Salmon River and tributaries, plus alpine lakes
Where: Frank Church–River of No Return Wilderness
The Fish: Steelhead, cutthroat, rainbow, and brook trout, arctic grayling
Access: Salmon, Idaho
Maps: Frank Church–River of No Return Wilderness
Overnight Possibilities: Yes, backpacking, rafting
Information Link: **www.fs.fed.us/r4/sc/recreation/fcronr**
Comments: At more than two million acres, you could get lost here for the summer.

The Water: Selway Wild and Scenic River, plus more than 100 alpine lakes
Where: Selway-Bitteroot Wilderness
The Fish: Chinook salmon, cutthroat, rainbow, bull, steelhead, and brook trout

Access: Grangeville, Idaho
Maps: Selway-Bitterroot Wilderness
Overnight
Possibilities: Yes, backpacking
Information Link: **www.fs.fed.us/r1/nezperce/wilderness**
Comments: Another huge Idaho wilderness with nearly endless potential for adventure.

Other potential Idaho destinations: Fish Creek, Sawtooth Wilderness, Gospel Hump Wilderness

Illinois

The Water: Hutchins Creek
Where: Bald Knob Wilderness
The Fish: Smallmouth bass, panfish
Access: Jonesboro, Illinois
Maps: Shawnee National Forest
Overnight
Possibilities: Yes, backpacking
Information Link: **www.fs.fed.us/r9/forests/shawnee**
Comments: Hutchins Creek is a Wild and Scenic River study candidate.

The Water: Lusk Creek
Where: Lusk Creek Wilderness
The Fish: Smallmouth bass, panfish
Access: Golconda, Illinois
Maps: Shawnee National Forest
Overnight
Possibilities: Yes, backpacking
Information Link: **www.fs.fed.us/r9/forests/shawnee**
Comments: One of the state's highest-quality streams.

Other potential Illinois destinations: Panther Den Wilderness, Saline River

Indiana

The Water: Wabash River
Where: Central and western Indiana
The Fish: Smallmouth and rock bass, catfish
Access: Wabash, Indiana
Maps: Indiana Gazetteer
Overnight
Possibilities: Yes, canoe camping
Information Link: **www.in.gov/dnr/outdoor/canoe/wabash**
Comments: Underutilized as a canoe camping river; has rural flavor, long trips possible.

The Water: Tippecanoe River
Where: Northern Indiana
The Fish: Pike, bass, panfish
Access: Rochester, Indiana
Maps: Indiana Gazetteer
Overnight
Possibilities: Yes, kayaking and canoeing
Information Link: **www.in.gov/dnr/outdoor/canoe/tippecan**
Comments: Spring-fed river is surprisingly clear.

Other potential Illinois destinations: Blue River, Whitewater River, Sugar Creek

Iowa

The Water: Paint Creek and Little Paint Creek
Where: Yellow River State Forest
The Fish: Trout
Access: Waterville, Iowa
Maps: Yellow River State Forest Trails Map
Overnight
Possibilities: Yes, backpacking
Information Link: **www.iowadnr.com/forestry/yellowriver**
Comments: Varied terrain and decent fishing for stocked trout.

The Water: Upper Iowa River
Where: Northeast Iowa
The Fish: Pike, smallmouth and rock bass, occasional stocked trout
Access: Decorah, Iowa
Maps: Iowa Gazetteer
Overnight
Possibilities: Yes, kayak and canoe camping
Information Link: **www.desmoinesriver.org/canoeguide/upperia.pdf**
Comments: Beautiful bluffs and springs will change your image of Iowa.

Other potential Iowa destinations: Yellow River, Shell Rock River, Big Sioux River

Kansas

The Water: Kansas River
Where: Eastern Kansas
The Fish: Crappie, catfish
Access: Topeka, Kansas
Maps: Kansas Gazetteer

Overnight
Possibilities: Yes, canoe camping
Information Link: **www.kansas.net/~tjhittle/kpg_vol2.html**
Comments: A total of 170 river miles to paddle.

Kentucky

The Water: Green River
Where: Mammoth Cave National Park
The Fish: Smallmouth bass, redeye, panfish
Access: Munfordville
Maps: Mammoth Cave National Park
Overnight
Possibilities: Yes, canoe camping and backpacking
Information Link: **www.nps.gov/maca**
Comments: Green River is a great touring river with fishing and camping possibilities inside and beyond Mammoth Cave National Park.

The Water: Kentucky Lake–Lake Barkley
Where: Land Between the Lakes National Recreation Area
The Fish: Largemouth and smallmouth bass, crappie, bream
Access: Twin Rivers, Kentucky
Maps: Land Between the Lakes National Recreation Area
Overnight
Possibilities: Yes, kayaking and canoeing
Information Link: **www.lbl.org**
Comments: Premier freshwater sea kayaking destination for anglers along shores of Land Between the Lakes.

Other potential Kentucky destinations: Big South Fork National River and Recreation Area, Cumberland River, Rockcastle River

Louisiana

The Water: Bogue Chitto River
Where: Southeastern Louisiana
The Fish: Largemouth bass, catfish, panfish
Access: Clifton, Louisiana
Maps: Louisiana Gazetteer
Overnight
Possibilities: Yes, kayak and canoe camping
Information Link: **members.aol.com/canoeboguechitto/index.html**
Comments: Touring portion of the river begins in South Mississippi and extends well into Louisiana.

The Water: Whiskey Chitto River
Where: Southwestern Louisiana
The Fish: Largemouth bass, panfish, catfish
Access: Mittie, Louisiana
Maps: Louisiana Gazetteer
Overnight
Possibilities: Yes, kayak and canoe camping
Information Link: **www.whiskeychitto.com**
Comments: Cool spring-fed waters and sandbars add appeal.

Other potential Louisiana destinations: Little River, Sabine River

Maine

The Water: Allagash River and adjoining lakes
Where: Allagash Wilderness Waterway
The Fish: Lake and brook trout, northern pike
Access: Ashland, Maine
Maps: Allagash Wilderness Waterway
Overnight
Possibilities: Yes, canoe camping
Information Link: **www.mainerivers.org/allagash**
Comments: The waterway is a combination of rivers and lakes that allow backcountry fishing trips up to 92 miles in length.

The Water: St. Croix River
Where: Maine–New Brunswick border
The Fish: Landlocked salmon, smallmouth bass
Access: Danforth, Maine
Maps: Maine Gazetteer
Overnight
Possibilities: Yes, canoeing
Information Link: **www.mainerivers.org/st_croix**
Comments: Multiple possibilities and lengths of trips in this river system that shares a border with New Brunswick.

Other potential Maine destinations: West Branch of the Penobscot River, East Branch of the Penobscot River, St. John River

Maryland

The Water: Fifteen Mile Creek
Where: Green Ridge State Forest
The Fish: Trout
Access: Cumberland, Maryland
Maps: Green Ridge State Forest

Backcountry Fishing

  Overnight
  Possibilities: Yes, backpacking
Information Link: **www.dnr.state.md.us**
  Comments: Trout are stocked on forest streams. Good backpacker's loop
    in combination with the old C&O Canal Towpath.

  The Water: Chincoteague Bay
  Where: Assateague Island National Seashore
  The Fish: Striped bass, sea trout, red drum
  Access: Ocean City, Maryland
  Maps: Assateague Island National Seashore
  Overnight
  Possibilities: Yes, kayaking, canoeing, and backpacking
Information Link: www.nps.gov/asis
  Comments: Travel the seashore by self-propelled craft or foot to
    designated backcountry campsites, and then surf-fish.

Other potential Maryland destinations: Savage River State Forest

Massachusetts

  The Water: Dunbar Brook
  Where: Monroe State Forest
  The Fish: Trout
  Access: Zoar, Massachusetts
  Maps: Monroe State Forest
  Overnight
  Possibilities: Yes, backpacking
Information Link: **www.mass.gov/dcr**
  Comments: This is also an early spring rafting run with campsites and
    shelters on the stream.

  The Water: Various forest brooks
  Where: Mount Washington State Forest
  The Fish: Trout
  Access: Sheffield, Massachusetts
  Maps: Mount Washington State Forest
  Overnight
  Possibilities: Yes, backpacking
Information Link: **www.mass.gov/dcr**
  Comments: Appalachian Trail travels through forest. Streams flow from
    Mount Washington.

Other potential Massachusetts destinations: Connecticut River

Michigan

The Water:	Manistique River
Where:	Upper Peninsula
The Fish:	Pike, walleye, smallmouth bass
Access:	Manistique, Michigan
Maps:	Michigan Gazetteer
Overnight Possibilities:	Yes, canoe and kayak camping
Information Link:	**www.northlandoutfitters.com**
Comments:	Can combine extended trip with Fox River and add trout.

The Water:	Manistee River
Where:	Manistee National Forest, Lower Peninsula
The Fish:	Steelhead, rainbow, and brook trout, salmon
Access:	Cadillac, Michigan
Maps:	Manistee National Forest
Overnight Possibilities:	Yes, kayaking and canoeing
Information Link:	**www.michigan.gov/dnr**
Comments:	Long river trips and big fish are possibilities.

Other potential Michigan destinations: Pine River, Au Sable River

Minnesota

The Water:	Boundary Waters Canoe Area Wilderness
Where:	Superior National Forest
The Fish:	Pike, walleye, smallmouth bass, lake trout, panfish
Access:	Ely, Minnesota
Maps:	Fischer Maps
Overnight Possibilities:	Yes
Information Link:	**www.fs.fed.us/r9/forests/superior/bwcaw**
Comments:	Arguably America's best canoe country—great paddling, camping, and fishing.

The Water:	Big Fork River
Where:	Manistee National Forest, Lower Peninsula
The Fish:	Walleye, northern pike, muskies
Access:	Grand Falls, Minnesota
Maps:	Minnesota Gazetteer
Overnight Possibilities:	Yes, canoeing
Information Link:	**dnr.state.mn.us**

Comments: River heads north through significant public land. Has good fishing and designated paddler campsites.

Other potential Minnesota destinations: Mississippi River, Zumbro River

Mississippi

The Water: Black Creek
Where: De Soto National Forest
The Fish: Largemouth bass, panfish, catfish
Access: Brooklyn, Mississippi
Maps: De Soto National Forest
Overnight Possibilities: Yes, by canoe, kayak, and backpack
Information Link: **www.fs.fed.us/r8/mississippi**
Comments: Consider hiking up the river, then floating back down. It's about 40 miles by water one-way or parallel hiking trail.

The Water: Chickasawhay River
Where: South Mississippi
The Fish: Bass, bream, catfish
Access: Shubuta, Mississippi
Maps: Mississippi Gazetteer
Overnight Possibilities: Yes, canoeing
Information Link: **www.mdwfp.com**
Comments: Long, lonely stretches of river and wildlife as well as fishing and camping.

Other potential Mississippi destinations: Pearl River, Pascagoula River, Bogue Chitto River

Missouri

The Water: Eleven Point River
Where: Mark Twain National Forest
The Fish: Rainbow trout, smallmouth bass, redeye, panfish
Access: Alton, Missouri
Maps: Mark Twain National Forest
Overnight Possibilities: Yes, by canoe, backpack
Information Link: **www.rivers.gov/wsr-eleven-point**
Comments: Massive springs cool sections of the Wild and Scenic River enough for trout-fishing. A great overall experience.

The fine scenery of Glacier National Park may distract you from the fishing.

The Water:	Current River–Jacks River
Where:	Ozark National Riverways
The Fish:	Trout, smallmouth bass, redeye, panfish
Access:	Eminence, Missouri
Maps:	Ozark National Riverways
Overnight Possibilities:	Yes, canoeing
Information Link:	**www.nps.gov/ozar**
Comments:	Run by National Park Service for recreational river use. Protected river corridor.

Other potential Missouri destinations: Gasconade River, Meramec River, North Fork White River

Montana

The Water:	Belly River and tributaries, including alpine lakes
Where:	Glacier National Park
The Fish:	Grayling; pike; salmon; cutthroat, rainbow, and brook trout
Access:	Whitefish, Montana
Maps:	Glacier National Park
Overnight Possibilities:	Yes, backpack

155

Information Link: **www.nps.gov/glac**
 Comments: The superlative scenery will distract you from the fine fishing.

 The Water: Middle Fork Flathead River and tributaries and high lakes
 Where: Great Bear Wilderness, Flathead National Forest
 The Fish: Bull and cutthroat trout
 Access: Hungry Horse, Montana
 Maps: Great Bear Wilderness
 Overnight
 Possibilities: Yes, backpacking
Information Link: **www.fs.fed.us/r1/flathead/wilderness**
 Comments: Great fishing in vast wilderness complex.

Other potential Mississippi destinations: Bob Marshall Wilderness, Mission Mountain Wilderness, Lee Metcalf Wilderness

Nebraska

 The Water: Niobrara River
 Where: North Central Nebraska
 The Fish: Pike, largemouth and smallmouth bass, white bass
 Access: Valentine, Nebraska
 Maps: Nebraska Gazetteer
 Overnight
 Possibilities: Yes, canoe
Information Link: **www.ngpc.state.ne.us**
 Comments: This federally designated Wild and Scenic River will surprise non-Nebraskans.

 The Water: Calamus River
 Where: Nebraska Sandhills
 The Fish: Pike, bass, catfish
 Access: Brewster, Nebraska
 Maps: Nebraska Gazetteer
 Overnight
 Possibilities: Yes, canoe camping
Information Link: **www.ngpc.state.ne.us**
 Comments: Once considered for Wild and Scenic designation. Fifty-six miles of paddleable river, designated campsites.

Other potential Nebraska destinations: Dismal River, Missouri River below Randall Creek

Nevada

The Water: Mosquito Creek and other streams and lakes of the Table Mountain Wilderness
Where: Toiyabe National Forest
The Fish: Cutthroat trout
Access: Belmont, Nevada
Maps: Tonopah Ranger District
Overnight Possibilities: Yes, backpacking
Information Link: **www.fs.fed.us/r4/htnf**
Comments: Five major streams lie within this 100,000-acre, high country wilderness.

The Water: Lakes and streams of the Ruby Mountains Wilderness
Where: Toiyabe National Forest
The Fish: Brook, rainbow, and Lahontan cutthroat trout
Access: Elko, Nevada
Maps: Ruby Mountains/East Humboldt Wilderness
Overnight Possibilities: Yes, backpacking
Information Link: **www.fs.fed.us/r4/htnf**
Comments: Two dozen lakes and many streams with plenty of trout.

Other potential Nevada destinations: East Humboldt Wilderness, Jarbidge Wilderness

New Hampshire

The Water: Umbagog Lake
Where: Umbagog Lake National Wildlife Refuge
The Fish: Brook and lake trout, smelt, smallmouth bass, salmon
Access: Errol, New Hampshire
Maps: Umbagog Lake National Wildlife Refuge
Overnight Possibilities: Yes, kayak and canoe camping
Information Link: **www.fws.gov/refuges**
Comments: Lots of wildlife in addition to fishing; must have camping permit. Plan ahead.

The Water: Wild River
Where: White Mountain National Forest
The Fish: Brook and rainbow trout, salmon
Access: Highwater Trail
Maps: White Mountain National Forest

Overnight
Possibilities: Yes, backpacking
Information Link: **www.fs.fed.us/r9/forests/white_mountain**
Comments: Start at the auto accessible Wild River Campground.

Other potential New Hampshire destinations: Connecticut River

New Jersey

The Water: Middle Delaware River
Where: Delaware Water Gap National Recreation Area
The Fish: Trout, smallmouth bass, shad
Access: Montague, New Jersey
Maps: Delaware Water Gap National Recreation Area
Overnight
Possibilities: Yes, kayak and canoe camping
Information Link: **www.nps.gov/dewa**
Comments: Forty miles of river, administered by the National Park Service, with designated campsites.

The Water: Pine Barrens
Where: Wharton State Forest
The Fish: Bass, pickerel, sunfish
Access: Pleasant Mills, New Jersey
Maps: New Jersey Gazetteer
Overnight
Possibilities: Yes, canoe camping
Information Link: **www.state.nj.us/pinelands**
Comments: Several paddleable rivers flow through the barrens, including two Wild and Scenic Waterways.

Other potential New Jersey destinations: Try different rivers within the Pine Barrens.

New Mexico

The Water: Upper Forks of the Gila River
Where: Gila Wilderness
The Fish: Trout, smallmouth bass
Access: Glenwood, New Mexico
Maps: Gila Wilderness
Overnight
Possibilities: Yes, backpacking
Information Link: **www2.srs.fs.fed.us/r3/gila**
Comments: Vast area, gorgeous river canyons, great fishing, hot springs. What more can you ask for?

The Water: Pecos River and adjacent lakes
Where: Pecos Wilderness
The Fish: Cutthroat, rainbow, and brown trout
Access: Penasco, New Mexico
Maps: Pecos Wilderness
Overnight
Possibilities: Yes, backpacking
Information Link: **www.fs.fed.us/r3/sfe**
Comments: Great fishing but can get busy.

Other potential New Mexico destinations: Wheeler Peak Wilderness, Chama River Canyon Wilderness

New York

The Water: Ponds and lakes of St. Regis Canoe Area
Where: Adirondacks
The Fish: Salmon, rainbow and lake trout
Access: Franklin County, New York
Maps: Adirondack Paddlers Map
Overnight
Possibilities: Yes, canoe camping
Information Link: **www.dec.state.ny.us**
Comments: Portages connect the 58 lakes and ponds.

The Water: West Canada Lakes Wilderness
Where: Adirondacks
The Fish: Brook trout
Access: Hamilton County, New York
Maps: Adirondack Park
Overnight
Possibilities: Yes, backpacking
Information Link: **www.adk.org**
Comments: More than 160,000 acres, 78 miles of trails, and more than 50 bodies of water.

Other potential New York destinations: Pharaoh Lake Wilderness, Five Ponds Wilderness

North Carolina

The Water: Hazel Creek and tributaries
Where: Great Smoky Mountains National Park
The Fish: Rainbow, brown, and brook trout
Access: Fontana Lake
Maps: Great Smoky Mountain National Park

Overnight
Possibilities: Yes, backpacking, kayak and canoe camping
Information Link: www.nps.gov/grsm
Comments: Either get boat shuttle or paddle to mouth of creek; designated campsites aplenty.

The Water: Slickrock Creek
Where: Nantahala National Forest
The Fish: Brown, rainbow, and brook trout
Access: Tapoco, North Carolina
Maps: Nantahala National Forest
Overnight
Possibilities: Yes, backpacking
Information Link: **www.cs.unca.edu/nfsnc**
Comments: Main creek and tributaries are pretty and have some good fishing.

Other potential North Carolina destinations: Santeelah Lake, Lumber River, Cape Lookout National Seashore.

North Dakota

The Water: Sheyenne River
Where: Eastern North Dakota
The Fish: Pike, perch, walleye, bass
Access: Fort Ransom, North Dakota
Maps: North Dakota Gazetteer
Overnight
Possibilities: Yes, canoe camping
Information Link: **www.ndparks.com/trails**
Comments: Long river displays wide variety of North Dakota landscapes.

The Water: Missouri River
Where: Central North Dakota
The Fish: Pike, walleye, brown and cutthroat trout
Access: Riverdale, North Dakota
Maps: North Dakota Gazetteer
Overnight
Possibilities: Yes, canoe camping
Information Link: **www.ndparks.com/trails**
Comments: Cold, clear river released from below from dam.

Other potential North Dakota destinations: Pembina River, Red River

Ohio

The Water:	Little Miami River
Where:	Near Cincinnati
The Fish:	Smallmouth and rock bass, panfish
Access:	Oregonia, Ohio
Maps:	Ohio Gazetteer
Overnight Possibilities:	Yes, kayak and canoe camping
Information Link:	**www.dnr.state.oh.us**
Comments:	Parts of river also have multiuse trail along it.

The Water:	Little Muskingum River
Where:	Wayne National Forest
The Fish:	Smallmouth bass, panfish, muskie
Access:	Marietta, Ohio
Maps:	Wayne National Forest
Overnight Possibilities:	Yes, canoe camping
Information Link:	**www.fs.fed.us/r9/wayne**
Comments:	Go in spring; has primitive campsites.

Other potential Ohio destinations: Symmes Creek, Pine Creek

Oklahoma

The Water:	Upper Kiamichi River Wilderness
Where:	Ouachita National Forest
The Fish:	Bass, panfish
Access:	Talihina, Oklahoma
Maps:	Ouachita National Forest
Overnight Possibilities:	Yes, backpacking
Information Link:	**www.fs.fed.us/r8/Ouachita**
Comments:	Seldom-fished azure waters.

The Water:	Illinois River
Where:	Northeastern Oklahoma
The Fish:	Bass, bream, walleye
Access:	Gore, Oklahoma
Maps:	Oklahoma Gazetteer
Overnight Possibilities:	Yes, canoe camping
Information Link:	**www.southwestpaddler.com**
Comments:	Good Ozark paddling and fishing in Oklahoma.

Other potential Oklahoma destinations: Mountain Fork River, Little River

Oregon

The Water:	Minam River and tributaries, alpine lakes
Where:	Eagle Cap Wilderness
The Fish:	Rainbow, golden, and brook trout
Access:	Minam, Oregon
Maps:	Eagle Cap Wilderness
Overnight Possibilities:	Yes, backpacking
Information Link:	**www.fs.fed.us/r6**
Comments:	Large areas of wilderness are rarely visited, lakes the busiest.

The Water:	North Fork John Day River and tributaries
Where:	North Fork John Day Wilderness
The Fish:	Rainbow and steelhead trout
Access:	Dale, Oregon
Maps:	Umatilla National Forest
Overnight Possibilities:	Yes, backpacking
Information Link:	**www.fs.fed.us/r6**
Comments:	Federally designated Wild and Scenic River.

Other potential Oregon destinations: North Fork Umatilla Wilderness, Rogue-Umpqua Divide Wilderness, Sky Lakes Wilderness

Pennsylvania

The Water:	Pine Creek
Where:	North-central Pennsylvania
The Fish:	Trout, smallmouth bass, panfish
Access:	Wellsboro, Pennsylvania
Maps:	Pennsylvania Gazetteer
Overnight Possibilities:	Yes, canoe camping
Information Link:	**www.pinecrk.com**
Comments:	Catch it in late spring to early summer for best floating.

The Water:	Allegheny River
Where:	Western Pennsylvania
The Fish:	Muskie, brown and rainbow trout
Access:	Warren, Pennsylvania
Maps:	Middle Allegheny River Water Trail
Overnight Possibilities:	Yes, canoe camping

Information Link: **www.fs.fed.us/r9/forests/allegheny/recreation/
water_activities**
    Comments: Large river with some civilization but great island camping
and big fish.

Other potential Pennsylvania destinations: Clarion River, Delaware River,
Youghiogheny River

South Carolina

    The Water: Chattooga River and tributaries
    Where: Ellicott Rock Wilderness
    The Fish: Rainbow, brown, and brook trout
    Access: Mountain Rest, South Carolina
    Maps: Ellicott Rock Wilderness
    *Overnight
Possibilities:* Yes, backpacking
Information Link: **www.fs.fed.us/r8/fms**
    Comments: Can be busy, but also can have big fish.

    The Water: Middle Saluda River
    Where: Jones Gap State Park
    The Fish: Brook and rainbow trout
    Access: Cleveland, South Carolina
    Maps: Mountain Bridge Wilderness
    *Overnight
Possibilities:* Yes, backpacking
Information Link: **www.southcarolinaparks.com**
    Comments: Well managed and gorgeous area, with designated
campsites.

Other potential South Carolina destinations: Broad River, Tyger River,
Enoree River

South Dakota

    The Water: Big Sioux River
    Where: Southeast South Dakota
    The Fish: Pike, walleye, catfish
    Access: Sioux Falls, South Dakota
    Maps: Big Sioux River Canoe/kayak map
    *Overnight
Possibilities:* Yes, kayak and canoe camping
Information Link: **www.sdgfp.info**
    Comments: Underutilized resource.

The Water:	Missouri River
Where:	South Central South Dakota
The Fish:	Bass, walleye
Access:	Pickstown, South Dakota
Maps:	Missouri River Canoe/kayak map
Overnight Possibilities:	Yes, kayak and canoe camping
Information Link:	**www.sdgfp.info**
Comments:	Start below Gavin's Point Dam for 59-mile stretch to Nebraska.

Other potential South Dakota destinations: Belle Fourche River, James River

Tennessee

The Water:	Upper Little River and tributaries
Where:	Great Smoky Mountains National Park
The Fish:	Rainbow, brown, and brook trout
Access:	Little River Trail
Maps:	Great Smoky Mountains National Park
Overnight Possibilities:	Yes, backpacking
Information Link:	**www.nps.gov/grsm**
Comments:	The best and most remote areas are farthest from the trailhead.

The Water:	Buffalo River
Where:	Middle Tennessee
The Fish:	Smallmouth and rock bass, panfish
Access:	Flatwoods, Tennessee
Maps:	Tennessee Gazetteer
Overnight Possibilities:	Yes, canoe camping
Information Link:	**www.crazyhorsecanoe.com**
Comments:	The Buffalo offers first-rate smallmouth-bass fishing in a beautiful setting.

Other potential Tennessee destinations: Land between the Lakes National Recreation Area, Citico Wilderness, Big South Fork National River and Recreation Area

Texas

The Water:	Sabine River
Where:	East Texas
The Fish:	Catfish, white bass, crappie

Access:	Burkeville, Texas
Maps:	Texas Gazetteer
Overnight Possibilities:	Yes, canoe camping
Information Link:	**www.sratx.org**
Comments:	Up to 150 miles of river to paddle. Plenty of sandbars for camping.

The Water:	Colorado River
Where:	East-central Texas
The Fish:	Largemouth and white bass, catfish
Access:	Austin, Texas
Maps:	Texas Gazetteer
Overnight Possibilities:	Yes, canoe camping
Information Link:	**www.southwestpaddler.com**
Comments:	River is best below Austin.

Other potential Texas destinations: Brazos River, Nueches River

Utah

The Water:	Rivers, streams and lakes of the High Uintas Wilderness
Where:	Ashley National Forest
The Fish:	Various trout
Access:	Kamas, Utah
Maps:	High Uintas Wilderness
Overnight Possibilities:	Yes, canoe camping
Information Link:	**www.fs.fed.us/r4/ashley**
Comments:	Nearly a half million acres of Utah Mountains to fish and explore.

The Water:	Streams of the highest Wasatch Mountains
Where:	Mount Nebo Wilderness
The Fish:	Rainbow trout
Access:	Nephi, Utah
Maps:	Uinta National Forest
Overnight Possibilities:	Yes, backpacking
Information Link:	**www.fs.fed.us/r4/uinta**
Comments:	The steep mountains have much biodiversity.

Other potential Utah destinations: Fish Creek, Virgin River east of Zion

Vermont

The Water:	Headwaters of White and New Haven rivers
Where:	Breadloaf Wilderness
The Fish:	Brook trout
Access:	East Middlebury, Vermont
Maps:	Green Mountain National Forest
Overnight Possibilities:	Yes, backpacking
Information Link:	**www.fs.fed.us/r9/gmfl**
Comments:	Old logging roads trace some of the drainages.

The Water:	Lake Champlain
Where:	Vermont–New York border
The Fish:	Trout, pike, bass
Access:	St. Albans Bay, Vermont
Maps:	Vermont Gazetteer
Overnight Possibilities:	Yes, kayak camping
Information Link:	www.lakechamplaincommittee.org
Comments:	More campsites are being developed on the lake's paddler trail.

Other potential Vermont destinations: Connecticut River

Virginia

The Water:	Big Run and tributaries
Where:	Shenandoah National Park
The Fish:	Brook trout
Access:	Waynesboro, Virginia
Maps:	Shenandoah National Park, South District
Overnight Possibilities:	Yes, backpacking
Information Link:	**www.nps.gov/shen**
Comments:	Big Run is just one of many backpack-fishing streams in the park.

The Water:	New River
Where:	Southwest Virginia
The Fish:	Smallmouth bass, walleye, muskie
Access:	Radford, Virginia
Maps:	Virginia Gazetteer
Overnight Possibilities:	Yes, canoe camping

Information Link: **dgif.state.va.us/fishing/waterbodies/display.asp?id=163**
Comments: Big valley, big fish, big touring river.

Other potential Virginia destinations: Mount Rogers National Recreation Area, James River, Rappahannock River

Washington

The Water: Wenaha River and tributaries
Where: Wenaha-Tucannon Wilderness
The Fish: Trout, salmon
Access: Troy, Washington
Maps: Wenaha-Tucannon Wilderness
Overnight
Possibilities: Yes, backpacking
Information Link: **www.fs.fed.us/r6/uma**
Comments: Little visited resource for backcountry anglers.

The Water: Ross Lake and tributaries
Where: North Cascades National Park/Recreation Area
The Fish: Trout
Access: Diablo, Washington
Maps: North Cascades map
Overnight
Possibilities: Yes, canoe, kayak and backpack camping
Information Link: **www.nps.gov/noca**
Comments: From Ross Lake you can combine paddle- and backpack-fishing in one trip.

Other potential Washington destinations: Pasayten Wilderness, Glacier Peak Wilderness, Olympic National Park

West Virginia

The Water: Williams River, North Fork Cranberry River
Where: Cranberry Backcountry and Wilderness
The Fish: Brown, rainbow, and brook trout
Access: Richwood, West Virginia
Maps: Monongahela National Forest
Overnight
Possibilities: Yes, backpacking
Information Link: **www.fs.fed.us/r9/mnf/sp/cranberrywilderness.html**
Comments: Bicyclists will be seen in the Cranberry Backcountry, pedaling to fish.

Backcountry Fishing

The Water: Seneca Creek
Where: Seneca Creek Backcountry
The Fish: Brook trout
Access: Elkins, West Virginia
Maps: Monongahela National Forest
Overnight Possibilities: Yes, backpacking
Information Link: **www.fs.fed.us/r9/mnf/rec/backcountry/seneca_creek_backcountry.htm**
Comments: Beautiful place in which to camp and fish for native brook trout.

Other potential West Virginia destinations: Laurel Fork Wilderness, Otter Creek Wilderness, Greenbrier River

Wisconsin

The Water: St. Croix River
Where: Northwestern Wisconsin
The Fish: Smallmouth bass, walleye, pike
Access: St. Croix Falls, Wisconsin
Maps: Saint Croix National Scenic Riverway
Overnight Possibilities: Yes, canoe, kayak camping
Information Link: **www.nps.gov/sacn**
Comments: Great smallmouth fishing and designated riverside sites.

The Water: Lower Wisconsin River
Where: Southwestern Wisconsin
The Fish: Smallmouth bass, walleye, muskie, panfish
Access: Spring Green, Wisconsin
Maps: Wisconsin Gazetteer
Overnight Possibilities: Yes, kayak and canoe camping
Information Link: **lwr.state.wi.us**
Comments: Large river has wild feel; can get busy on summer weekends.

Other potential Wisconsin destinations: Black River, Red Cedar River, Namekagon River

Wyoming

The Water: Slough Creek
Where: Yellowstone National Park
The Fish: Cutthroat trout

Access:	Cooke City, Montana
Maps:	Yellowstone National Park
Overnight Possibilities:	Yes, backpack camping
Information Link:	**www.nps.gov/yell**
Comments:	Majestic scenery and meadow-fishing. Many other destinations exist at Yellowstone.

The Water:	Cloud Peak Wilderness
Where:	Big Horn National Forest
The Fish:	Rainbow and brook trout
Access:	Sheridan, Wyoming
Maps:	Cloud Peak Wilderness
Overnight Possibilities:	Yes, backpack camping
Information Link:	**www.fs.fed.us/r2/bighorn/recreation/wilderness**
Comments:	High country. Good fishing on lakes and streams.

Other potential Wisconsin destinations: Bridger Wilderness, Fitzpatrick Wilderness, Grand Teton National Park

Appendixes

A Backpack-fishing Story

May is an exciting time to be in the Great Smoky Mountains National Park. The weather becomes milder, the streams warm up to merely bone-chilling cold, and the fish begin to feed. For the trout angler, the winter wait is over. The lures and flies have been assembled; the instructional books have been reread once again. It is now time for action.

More than 700 miles of fishable streams flow through the Smokies. Roads parallel many of these streams, affording easy access. But this accessibility has drawbacks. Too many anglers in a stream make the trout even more skittish and cautious than normal. And having a road nearby detracts from the scenic value of the experience; the sight and sound of cars droning by negates the get-away-from-it-all mountain experience. I personally find it irritating when auto tourists stop and watch me fish. I feel under pressure to catch one for them, which almost never happens. And when one car stops, other cars pull over to see what the first car stopped to see, and before long you'll be fishing for an audience.

But backcountry trails lead to and parallel other streams, eliminating the auto tourist audience and many anglers who aren't willing to hike for a head-to-head battle with the wary trout. And finally, some streams flow through trackless wilderness where the fisher must match wits against unknown terrain as well as the elusive quarry. With this in mind, my adventurous hiking friend John Cox and I opted for the two-pronged challenge of off-trail hiking and trout-fishing in Panther Creek.

It was already 6 p.m. when we arrived at the park border. John and I promptly began a hand-over-foot climb along a noisy little rivulet and traversed a tiny gap—our gateway into the Panther Creek watershed. Soon the rushing sounds of Panther Creek harkened our arrival at the old railroad grade abreast of the stream. Gray, pocked, water worn boulders and the crashing whitewater stood out in bold relief as we found an ideal out-of-the-way fishing camp.

After our evening meal, we reclined by the fire, discussing our fishing strategies for the next day. Before we knew it morning was upon us.

Backcountry Fishing

John made a monster batch of buckwheat pancakes, syrup and butter laden, which we washed down with rich, nearly scalding coffee.

Full and satisfied, I left camp with rod in hand, moving upstream to fish. John hiked way upstream. A chill crept over me while fishing. The densely forested, trailless banks forced me to travel through the cold water. Unfortunately my luck was less satisfying than the awesome splendor of the spring scenery. The trees and other plants looked so vibrant it seemed as if I could see them growing and greening before my eyes. Though I tried several different lures, several hours and many casts later I had netted just two puny rainbows, returned to the stream. I dejectedly trudged back to camp.

John loitered about our campsite, announcing he'd been shut out. It was 5 p.m. already and we had meager fixings for dinner. I decided to head down river and try my hand on the lower reaches of Panther Creek, where I'd been lucky before. Within five minutes, I hooked the largest rainbow I'd ever pulled out of that creek. It was easily over a foot long and had been fished out of a tiny pool not much bigger than the fish itself. Trout are hard to figure out because they feed with maddening irregularity. This adds to the challenge of fishing for them, but can tax the angler's sanity. In short order I had nabbed three more healthy trout. By 6 o'clock I was striding back to camp proudly toting our evening fare. Dusk came as we feasted on sautéed trout and baked beans. The lantern brightened our corner of the woods as we whiled away the hours discussing the pitfalls and joys of trout-fishing in the Smokies.

We awoke at dawn to the sound of chirping birds, having slept in the open, cool air. As usual, a night under the stars left me feeling especially invigorated. Next morning, we stalked off trail through dense, untracked timberland up the creek, arriving at the next camp late that afternoon. Before I could get my pack off, John hurriedly grabbed his rod and jumped in the water. He positioned himself at the base of a large pool upstream, below a drop where the creek narrowed, flanked on the left by a large boulder. He cast into a riffle at the head of the deep pool and let it sink to a count of five, then retrieved it slowly. He had no takers, but cast again.

Suddenly his line ran counter to the current. Adrenaline pulsed through his veins as he set the hook and landed a defiant rainbow. He unhooked the trout and shakily ran a cord through his lower lip, then tied the cord onto the belt loop of his pants. Continuing to work the pool, he landed another trout and two rock bass, releasing the bass, and moved on beyond the camp.

I headed downstream from camp and fished my way back. A faint fisherman's trail shadows the creek, which I followed. My struggle that led through rhododendron thickets, over fallen trees, and amid poking branches was made more difficult by having a fishing rod in one hand and a stringer of trout in the other. Finally I spotted the flickering firelight across the stream, marking the campsite. After fording Panther Creek in total darkness I saw John tending the welcoming fire. He recapped his day while slicing onions and potatoes for hash browns. I cleaned the trout and dipped them in a plastic freezer bag full of cornmeal. Soon the aroma of frying fresh trout permeated our camp as I put away the resealable bag of meal for future use. Shortly we dined on tasty breaded trout, steamy hash browns, strong hot coffee, and cool mountain water. Neither John nor I said, "It doesn't get any better than this." That went without saying.

We awoke to a cloudy sky. Our packs were much lighter on our departure than when we had entered the forest. We left Panther Creek via a gap and came out on a road at the edge of the park. A friendly local came along and gave us a lift in the bed of his ancient Ford pickup, carrying us back to my vehicle. That short, quiet ride in the old truck bed, the wind blowing about us, provided our reentry into the "outside" world, beyond the forests and mountains.

Backcountry Day-hike Fishing Checklist

Considerations: Where to go?
Type of fish, ability limits of party
Resources: State forests and parks, national forests and parks
When to go? What fish are biting when, weather, season

Fishing:
___ Rod and reel
___ Lures/flies
___ Extra line
___ Leader
___ Hemostats
___ Clippers
___ Stringer
___ Fishing license

Shoes:
___ Fishing shoes, hiking shoes

Clothes:
___ Dress in layers
___ Jacket/poncho
___ Hat
___ Extra clothes as needed or desired

Other Stuff:
___ Map
___ Compass
___ Lighter
___ Fire starter
___ Medical kit
___ Toilet paper
___ Knife
___ Headlamp
___ Food
___ Water or drinks

Other items to consider: Eyeglasses, bug dope, trash bag, camera, watch, sunscreen, lip balm, GPS, weather radio, sunglasses, binoculars, wildlife identification books

Backcountry Day-paddler Fishing Checklist

Considerations: Where to go?
Type of fish, paddle ability of party
Resources: Paddleable fishing rivers, lakes, and coastal areas
When to go? What fish are biting when, weather, season

Fishing:

___Rod and reel

___Full tackle box

___Second rod and reel

___Lures/flies

___Extra line

___Leader

___Hemostats/pliers

___Clippers

___Stringer

___Fish glove

___Fishing license

Boat:

___Canoe/kayak

___Paddles

___Spare paddle

___Personal flotation device

___Dry bags for gear storage

___Whistle

___Tow line

___Bilge pump for kayak

___Spray skirt for kayak

___Paddle float/lanyard for kayak

___Maps, charts, and tide tables

___Throw lines

___Boat sponge

Shoes:

___River shoes

Clothes:

___Wide brimmed hat

___Sun/cold protection clothes

___Jacket/poncho

___Extra clothes in a dry bag

___Sunglasses with strap

Other stuff:

___Compass

___Weather radio

___Sunscreen

___Lip balm

___Lighter

___Medical kit

___Toilet paper

___Knife

___Headlamp

___Cooler

___Food, including a little extra food

___Drinks

Other items to consider: Eyeglasses, bug dope, trash bag, aspirin, camera, watch, GPS, binoculars, flora/fauna identification books

Backcountry Backpack-fishing Checklist

Considerations: Where to go?
Physical ability, fishing expectations, trip expectations
Type of fish, time limits of party
Resources: State forests and parks, national forests and parks
When to go? What fish are biting when, weather, season

Fishing:
__ Rod and reel
__ Lures
__ Extra line
__ Hemostats
__ Clippers
__ Stringer
__ Fishing license

Shoes:
__ Fishing shoes, hiking shoes, camp shoes

Clothes:
__ Dress in layers
__ Socks
__ Long pants
__ Short pants
__ T-shirt
__ Long-sleeve shirt
__ Vest
__ Jacket/poncho
__ Extra clothes as needed or desired

Bedroom:
__ Closed-cell sleeping pad
__ Ultralight air mattress
__ Sleeping bag
__ Pillow

Bathroom:
__ Toothbrush/paste/floss
__ Toilet paper
__ Lotion
__ Biodegradable soap
__ Pills as needed

Other Stuff:
— Maps
— Compass
— Lighter
— Fire starter
— Medical kit
— Knife
— Rope—enough to hang food from bears
— Headlamp

Other items to consider: Eyeglasses, lantern/candles, bug dope, trash bag, GPS, weather radio, aspirin, book, radio, camera, cards, vitamins, watch, sunscreen, lip balm, extra batteries, sunglasses, small towel, trowel, paper plates, binoculars, wildlife identification books, paper towels

Roof: Tent, tarp or under the stars
Kitchen:
Food: Food, spices
Water Purification: Filter, tablets, boil
Cookware: Cup, spoon, pot, pot holder, frying pan, spatula
Heat Sources: Stove or fire/grill

Backcountry Fishing Paddle-camp Checklist

Considerations: Where to go?
Paddling ability, fishing expectations, trip expectations
Type of fish, ability limits of party
Resources: Touring rivers, lakes, and coastal areas
When to go? What fish are biting when, weather, season

Fishing:
— Rod and reel
— Second rod and reel
— Lures/flies
— Extra line
— Leader
— Reel oil
— Hemostats/pliers
— Clippers
— Stringer
— Fish glove
— Fishing license

Boat:
— Canoe/kayak
— Paddles
— Spare paddle
— Personal flotation device
— Dry bags for gear storage
— Whistle
— Tow line
— Bilge pump for kayak
— Spray skirt for kayak
— Paddle float/lanyard for kayak
— Maps, charts, and tide tables
— Throw lines
— Boat sponge

Clothes:
— Dress in layers

Shoes:
— Boating shoes, camp shoes
— Socks
— Long pants
— Short pants

—T-shirt
—Long-sleeve shirt
—Vest
—Jacket/poncho
—Rain suit
—Extra clothes as needed or desired

Bedroom:
—Closed-cell sleeping pad
—Ultralight air mattress
—Sleeping bag
—Pillow

Bathroom:
—Toothbrush/paste/floss
—Toilet paper
—Lotion
—Biodegradable soap
—Pills as needed

Other Stuff:
—Compass
—Lighter
—Weather radio
—Fire starter
—Medical kit
—Knife
—Cooler
—Rope (enough to hang food up and away from bears)
—Headlamp

Other items to consider: Lantern/candles, eyeglasses, bug dope, trash bag, GPS, weather radio, aspirin, book, radio, camera, cards, vitamins, watch, sunscreen, lip balm, extra batteries, sunglasses, small towel, trowel, paper plates, binoculars, wildlife identification books, paper towels

Roof: Tent and/or tarp or under the stars, cord for tarp
Kitchen:
Food: food, spices
Water Purification: Filter, tablets, boils
Cookware: cup, spoon, fork, pot, pot holder, frying pan, spatula
Heat Sources: Stove or fire/grill

Other Backcountry Fishing Resources/Schools

There are several ways to learn the art of backcountry fishing. You can learn from your family members, go with other anglers, read this book, join a fishing organization, or go to fishing school. Fishing schools can be helpful for both the novice and experienced fisher. Not only do you learn a thing or two, you get to mingle with like-minded enthusiasts. And you will likely be in beautiful settings, making for a good activity all the way around. The fees can range from low to high depending upon whether you are getting group or individual instruction, and whether meals and lodging are included. There are schools throughout the United States, so there is likely one near you. Do an Internet search to find a nearby fishing school and may your degree be a whopper.

Also consider joining a fishing organization, such as Trout Unlimited. Fishing organizations are organized on various levels from national to statewide to local. These groups not only promote fishing but also conservation and expansion of the resource. Once again you will find yourself in the midst of like-minded individuals who love backcountry fishing as much as we do.

Index

181

About the Author

Johnny Molloy is an outdoor writer based in Johnson City, Tennessee. Born in Memphis, he moved to Knoxville in 1980 to attend the University of Tennessee. During his college years, he developed a love of the natural world that has become the primary focus his life.

It all started on a backpacking foray into Great Smoky Mountains National Park. That first trip was a disaster; nevertheless, Johnny discovered a love of the outdoors that would lead him to canoe-camp and backpack throughout the United States and abroad over the next 25 years. Today, he averages 150 nights out per year.

After graduating from UT in 1987 with a degree in economics, Johnny spent an ever-increasing amount of time in the wild, becoming more skilled in a variety of environments. Friends enjoyed his adventure stories; one even suggested that he write a book. He pursued that idea and soon parlayed his love of the outdoors into an occupation.

The results of his efforts are more than 30 books, including hiking, camping, paddling, and other comprehensive guidebooks, as well as books on true outdoor adventures. He has also written numerous articles for magazines and Web sites, and he continues to write and travel extensively to all four corners of the United States, endeavoring in a variety of outdoor pursuits. For the latest on Johnny, visit his Web site, **www .johnnymolloy.com.**